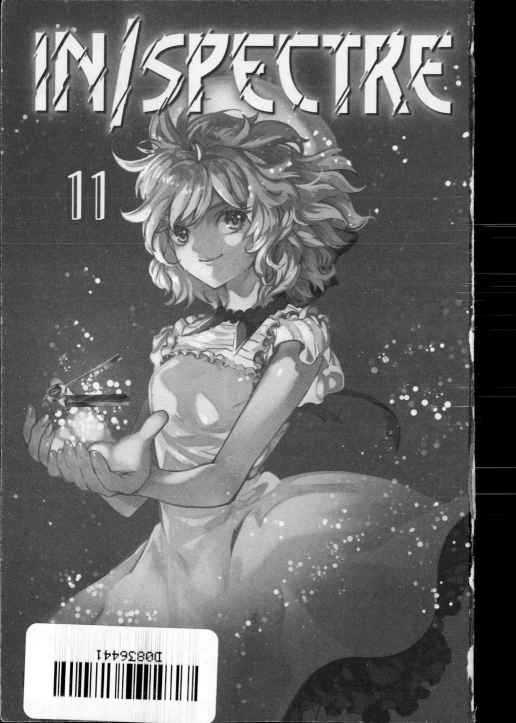

IN/SPECTRE
11

CONTENTS

IN/SPECTRE SLEEPING MURDER ARC

ASSIGNMENT & CHARACTER DIAGRAM

CHAIRMAN GÔICHI OTONASHI'S ASSIGNMENT:

I killed my wife Sumi-san 23 years ago. Explain how that is true.

REWARD

Whoever accomplishes the assignment best will be given priority when selecting the Chairman's assets for inheritance.

GÔICHI OTONASHI

The man who gave this assignment. Hired a fox spirit to murder Sumi 23 years ago.

23 years ago

SUMI OTONASHI

Assassinated 23 years ago. Was president of the Otonashi Group.

RYÔMA OTONASHI (ELDEST SON)

Currently a chef.

23 years ago

KAORUKO OTONASHI (ELDEST DAUGHTER)

Married to Kôya Fujinuma.

23 years ago

SUSUMU OTONASHI (SECOND SON)

Executive director of the Otonashi Group.

23 years ago

REPRESENTED BY

RION OTONASHI

Ryôma's daughter.

REPRESENTED BY

KÔYA FUJINUMA

Kaoruko's husband.

REPRESENTED BY

SUSUMU OTONASHI (HIMSELF)

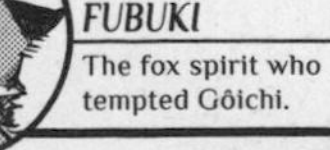

FUBUKI

The fox spirit who tempted Gôichi.

KOTOKO IWANAGA

The judge of this assignment.

KURÔ SAKURAGAWA

Kotoko's attendant.

IN/SPECTRE

I NEVER KNEW MY GRAND-FATHER VERY WELL. I ONLY SAW HIM A FEW TIMES A YEAR.
EVEN THOUGH HE'S THE CHAIR-MAN AND CEO OF A GLOBAL HOTEL CHAIN,
AND I'M THE DAUGH-TER OF HIS ELDEST SON...
Happy New Year, Rion.
...MY FATHER STRUCK OUT ON HIS OWN AND OPENED A SMALL JAPANESE RESTAURANT.
SO I WAS BORN AND RAISED A COM-MONER.
TUG
きゅ

MY FATHER TELLS ME THAT WHEN HE WAS YOUNG, HE WAS MADE TO LIVE AN ELITE LIFESTYLE AS AN EXECUTIVE AND FUTURE OWNER OF A LARGE CORPORATION...

ZSH

...AND MAYBE IT WAS A REBELLIOUS SPIRIT THAT MADE HIM ASPIRE TO THE LIFE OF AN ARTISAN INSTEAD.

CHOP

CHOP

CHOP

HE AND UNCLE SUSUMU—THE MAN WHO DID TAKE OVER THE COMPANY—ARE POLAR OPPOSITES.

THAT MIGHT BE WHY THEY NEVER GOT ALONG.

He's nice to me, though.

IF SOMETHING HAD GONE DIFFERENTLY, I MIGHT HAVE ENDED UP THE PROUD HEIRESS TO THE OTONASHI GROUP.

ZSHHH

IT DOES SOUND LIKE A RESTRICTIVE LIFE.

ZSHHH

DAD CAME TO ME WITH A BIZARRE ASSIGN-MENT.
RION.
I WANT YOU TO DO THIS FOR ME.
Otonashi Family Inheritance
RESOURCE FILE

AT ANY RATE, IT'S ABOUT THE MURDER 23 YEARS AGO. HE PROBABLY KNOWS SOMETHING THAT THE REST OF US DON'T—
SOMETHING THAT HE CAN TELL US NOW THAT SO MUCH TIME HAS PASSED. BUT HE WANTS US TO FIGURE IT OUT.

RUSTLE
DAD SAYS HE WANTS TO SHOW US THAT CRIMES WILL ALWAYS BE PUNISHED.
nheritance

IF YOU GET THE PRIORITY FOR THE INHERITANCE, YOU CAN DO WHATEVER YOU WANT WITH IT.
FLOP
FLOP

FLOP
FLOP

CHAPTER 26: "SLEEPING MURDER PART TWO"

ONE OF MY RELATIVES WAS THE VICTIM OF A MURDER.
NOW I'M SUPPOSED TO EXPLAIN HOW MY GRAND-FATHER WAS THE KILLER.
AND THERE'S A HUGE INHERI-TANCE ON THE LINE.
NONE OF THIS FEELS REAL.
AS FAR AS THE INHERITANCE GOES, I CAN'T SEE IT BEING ANYTHING BUT TROUBLE.
AND I FEEL EXTREMELY UNDER-DRESSED.
SO...
LOUNGE
EVERY-ONE.
THANK YOU FOR COMING.

THE SCHEMES OF AN OLD MAN WITH MONEY, POWER, AND BRAINS DO MAKE LIFE DIFFICULT FOR THE REST OF US, DON'T YOU AGREE?

I'M SURE YOU ALL HAVE QUESTIONS ABOUT ME: "WHO ARE YOU?" "WHAT ARE YOU DOING HERE?"
"WHAT SORTS OF VILE DEEDS ARE YOU PARTY TO?"

I HAVE NOTHING TO DO WITH ANY OF THIS.
AND YET I AM ORDERED TO ASSUME THIS BIZARRE ROLE, FORCING ME TO TAKE TIME OUT OF MY SCHEDULE TO COME ALL THE WAY TO THIS HOTEL.

BUT THINK ABOUT IT FOR A MOMENT.
I AM THE ONE MOST PUT OUT IN ALL THIS.

YOU MAY BE THINKING I COULD HAVE REFUSED IF IT WAS SUCH A PROBLEM, BUT COULD *YOU* REFUSE A REQUEST FROM *THE* CHAIRMAN OTONASHI?
WELL, I DO SEE WHERE SHE'S COMING FROM...

FURTHERMORE, I AM TO EVALUATE AND RANK YOU. NO MATTER WHAT I DO, WHOEVER COMES OUT ON BOTTOM WILL HOLD IT AGAINST ME.
THERE'S NO TELLING WHAT SORT OF RETALIATION I WILL BE FORCED TO FACE IN THE FUTURE.
OH, NO.
SURELY YOU DON'T THINK WE WOULD BE THAT PETTY.
BESIDES, DAD WOULDN'T ALLOW IT.

YOU MEN HAVE DONE SOME BACK-GROUND CHECKS ON ME, NO?

I TRIED, BUT NONE OF THE DETECTIVE AGENCIES I TRUST WERE WILLING TO DO IT.

THAT ALONE MAKES IT VERY CLEAR THAT THERE'S SOMETHING UNUSUAL ABOUT YOU.
THEY UNANI-MOUSLY AGREED THAT I SHOULD LEAVE THE IWANAGA HEIRESS ALONE.

I ACTUALLY HAPPEN TO HAVE A NEPHEW WHO WAS IN YOUR CLUB IN HIGH SCHOOL.

MANABU AMACHI. DO YOU REMEMBER HIM?
HE WARNED ME TO AVOID GETTING ON YOUR BAD SIDE AT ALL COSTS.

OH!
YOU WERE A RELATIVE OF MY CLUB PRESI-DENT?

How strange.
I WOULD HAVE EXPECTED HIM TO SPEAK MORE FAVORABLY ABOUT ME.
Oh, no.
PLEASE DON'T BE OFFENDED—MANABU MEANT NO ILL WILL.

...BOY-FRIEND?

AND IT'S NOT EVERY DAY THAT I GET TO GO TO SUCH A LOVELY HOTEL WITH HIM.

NATURALLY, I WANT TO TAKE MY TIME AND ENJOY IT!

ぱあっ BEEEAM

SPARKLE
キラ
THE SUITE THAT WAS RESERVED FOR MY LODGINGS HAS AN ENORMOUS BATHROOM.
I THOUGHT WE'D GET IN THE BATH, START WITH A NICE TUNNEL WASH...
...AND THEN DO ALL KINDS OF OTHER FUN THINGS TOGETHER!
BFFT!
BWOFF
キラ
SPARKLE

MMMMPH!
FLAIL
UNCLE, WHAT'S A "TUNNEL WASH"?
FLAIL

OH, UM.
AHEM
I BELIEVE KÔYA-SAN WOULD BE MORE KNOWLEDGE-ABLE ABOUT THAT SORT OF THING.
?
ちら
GLANCE
THAT'S NOT FAIR, HIDING BEHIND ME, SUSUMU-SAN.

EXCUSE ME. I DIDN'T MEAN TO BE SO VOCAL ABOUT MY PERSONAL INTERESTS.
YOU SEE, WE WENT TO A HOT SPRING RECENTLY, BUT WE WERE NOT ABLE TO BATHE TOGETHER.

...TO SPEND THE NEXT 24 HOURS IN NEGOTIATIONS, INSINUATIONS, AND PARANOIA.
AT ANY RATE, I'M SURE YOU ALL AGREE THAT IT WOULD BE LESS THAN IDEAL...
TRUE. AND I'M NOT EXCITED ABOUT THE IDEA OF MAKING MY FAMILY RELATIONS WORSE.
CLAP
SO I SUGGEST WE FORM AN ALLIANCE.

A—
ALLI-ANCE ...?

CHAIRMAN OTONASHI HAS ASKED YOU TO EXPLAIN HOW IT WAS THAT *HE* KILLED SUMI OTONASHI-SAN 23 YEARS AGO.
I SUGGEST WE ALL WORK TOGETHER TO COME UP WITH ONE ANSWER FOR HIM.

WE CAN ALSO DISCUSS THE DISTRIBUTION OF THE INHERITANCE,
THEN I WILL RANK YOU IN ORDER SUCH THAT EVERYONE GETS WHAT THEY WANT.
AND I WILL TELL THE CHAIRMAN THAT THE RANKINGS ARE BASED ON HOW MUCH EACH OF YOU CONTRIBUTED TO OUR SINGLE ANSWER.

I MEAN, REALLY,
IT WOULD BE SO TIRING TO HAVE TO LISTEN TO THREE SEPARATE ANSWERS.
I WILL LEAVE FOR APPROXIMATELY ONE HOUR.

PLEASE USE THAT TIME TO DISCUSS MY PROPOSAL.
SHUT
バタ
DID DAD TELL HER TO MAKE THAT SUGGES-TION...OR DID SHE COME UP WITH IT?
I DOUBT THAT. SHE WOULDN'T IGNORE THE CHAIRMAN'S WISHES.
I DON'T KNOW. IT SEEMS TO ME LIKE SHE'D DO THAT WITHOUT A SECOND THOUGHT.
WELL.
THE IDEA ITSELF ISN'T A BAD ONE.
IN FACT, IT MAKES SENSE.
SO WHAT ARE YOUR OPINIONS ABOUT THE INHERI-TANCE?

PERSONALLY, THERE ARE CERTAIN ASSETS I WOULD LIKE TO CLAIM THE RIGHTS TO.
MY WIFE AND CHILDREN HAD SOME REQUESTS FOR THE INHERITANCE, AND I HAVE TO TAKE THOSE INTO CONSIDERATION, TOO.
BUT IF I'M GUARANTEED THOSE THINGS, THEN I DON'T CARE WHAT RANK I GET IN THE ASSIGNMENT.
WHAT ABOUT KAORUKO-NÊSAN?
SHE SAYS THAT SHE'S NOT INTERESTED IN LETTING YOU AND RYÔMA-SAN GET ALL THE PROFIT.
ESPECIALLY SINCE YOU'RE THE CHAIRMAN'S FAVORITE, WORKING FOR THE GROUP AND ALL,
AND RYÔMA-SAN GETS A LOT OF RESPECT FOR HAVING THE GUTS TO FOLLOW HIS OWN PATH IN A COMPLETELY OPPOSITE DIRECTION.
ON THE OTHER HAND, KAORUKO SEEMS TO FEEL LIKE HER FATHER DOESN'T LOVE HER VERY MUCH.
IF THE TWO OF YOU WERE GIVEN PREFERENCE IN THE INHERITANCE, I DON'T THINK SHE COULD TAKE IT.

YOU KNOW, KÔYA-SAN, IF YOU WOULD USE THE OTONASHI GROUP TO HELP YOUR OWN BUSINESS, IT WOULD GIVE DAD AN OPPORTUNITY TO BE MORE INVOLVED WITH KAORUKO-NÊSAN.
YES, BUT I HAVE *MY* PRIDE, TOO.
I DON'T WANT PEOPLE ATTRIBUTING MY SUCCESS TO THE POWER OF THE OTONASHI.

BESIDES, KAORUKO DOCON'T CARE ABOUT MONEY.
I MAY BE A COMPETENT BUSINESS OWNER NOW,
BUT WHEN SHE MARRIED ME, OUR FINANCIAL PROSPECTS WERE FAR FROM PROMISING.
HMPH.
SO SHE JUST WANTS THE SATISFAC-TION OF KNOWING SHE BEAT HER BROTHERS.

OR MAYBE IN THIS CASE, SHE MAY WANT TO SHOW EVERYONE THAT SHE CHOSE A HUSBAND WHO'S BETTER THAN BOTH OF US.
WELL, THE TWO OF YOU *ARE* BRILLIANT MEN.
KAORUKO IS RATHER INSECURE ABOUT THAT, TOO.

WHAT DID RYÔMA-SAN SAY ABOUT THE INHERITANCE?

AS IF YOU EVEN NEEDED TO ASK.

INHERITING A LARGE SUM OF MONEY WILL BRING NOTHING BUT TROUBLE.
BUT IF RION WANTS ANYTHING, SHE SHOULD MAKE SURE TO GET IT. I BET THAT'S WHAT HE SAID.

IF YOU KNOW DAD THAT WELL, UNCLE SUSUMU, THEN WHY DO YOU STILL HATE HIM SO MUCH?

BE-CAUSE I KNOW HIM SO WELL.
HE ALWAYS DOES EXACTLY WHAT I DON'T WANT HIM TO DO.
TMP
TMP

IF THE ELDEST GIVES UP THE INHERITANCE, OR IF I GET MORE THAN MY "FAIR" SHARE, PEOPLE WILL START TO SUSPECT THINGS.
SOME MAY CLAIM I RIGGED THE CONTEST.
Oh...

DOES HE HAVE ANY IDEA HOW MUCH WORK I HAVE TO DO, CLEANING UP HIS MESSES AND CUTTING RED TAPE FOR HIM?
I'M SURE HE'S JUST HAPPY DOING EVERY-THING HE EVER WANTED TO DO.
IRK
IRK
IRK

AH... SORRY ABOUT THAT.

GASP
OH, IT'S NOT YOUR FAULT, RION.
IT'S ALL *HIS* FAULT.

THEN FOR THE RANKINGS, WE'LL PUT UNCLE KÔYA IN FIRST PLACE,
TO MAKE AUNT KAORUKO LOOK GOOD.

AS FOR WHAT *YOU* INHERIT, WOULD IT BE BEST FOR YOU AND UNCLE KÔYA TO DISCUSS WHAT YOU WANT, AND WE CAN MAKE SURE YOU BOTH GET IT?
BECAUSE I DON'T CARE WHAT RANK I GET.

I DON'T HAVE ANY PROBLEMS WITH THAT, AND I'M SURE KAORUKO WOULD BE HAPPY WITH IT.
WHAT ABOUT YOU, SU-SUMU-SAN?

IT'S EASIER TO DO IT THIS WAY THAN TO COMPETE OVER WHO HAS A BETTER ANSWER.
I DIDN'T WANT TO FIGHT OVER THE INHERITANCE TO BEGIN WITH.

...BUT *IS* THERE A RIGHT ANSWER TO THIS ASSIGNMENT?

IF GRANDFATHER IS TRYING TO ATONE IN SOME WAY BY LETTING US KNOW ABOUT HIS CRIME,

THEN WOULDN'T IT BE FASTER TO JUST TELL US HOW HE DID IT?

WHY IS HE MAKING *US* COME UP WITH THE SOLUTION?

DO YOU THINK HE HAD SOMETHING ELSE IN MIND WHEN HE GAVE THE ASSIGNMENT?
GRANDFATHER PROBABLY KNOWS SOMETHING THAT THE REST OF US DON'T, AND NOW THAT ENOUGH TIME HAS PASSED, HE WANTS US TO FIGURE IT OUT.
THAT'S WHAT DAD SAID...
...
EVEN IF WE DO ACCEPT THE YOUNG LADY'S PROPOSAL, THERE ARE A FEW THINGS THAT NEED SOME CLARIFICATION.
OH, PLEASE, YOU'RE OVERTHINKING THIS.
CHAIRMAN OTONASHI IS INVOLVED IN HIS WIFE'S DEATH.
BUT HE DOESN'T THINK YOU WOULD BELIEVE HIM IF HE TOLD YOU HOW HE DID IT.
SO HE WANTS YOU, HIS CHILDREN, TO COME TO THE CONCLUSION ON YOUR OWN, THAT'S ALL.
MUNCH

AND...

WE CAN TRUST YOU ON THIS?

THERE *IS* A RIGHT ANSWER.

AND IF YOU ALL SEEK OUT THE TRUTH, YOU WILL FIND IT.

BUT THERE'S NO REASON TO SUSPECT DAD.

ARE YOU SURE ABOUT THAT?

SNAP

THINK, FOR EXAMPLE, ABOUT THE PEOPLE CLOSE TO THE CASE THAT CHAIRMAN OTONASHI WOULD NOT WANT TO FALL UNDER SUSPICION.
RYÔMA-SAN, KAORUKO-SAN, SUSUMU-SAN, KÔYA-SAN.
DON'T YOU THINK IT'S ODD THAT EVERY ONE OF YOU HAD AN ALIBI?

ALMOST AS IF SOMEONE HAD TAKEN STEPS TO PROTECT YOU.

AT THE TIME, ONLY CHAIRMAN OTONASHI WAS POWERFUL ENOUGH TO HAVE ACCOMPLISHED SUCH A THING, WOULDN'T YOU AGREE?

THE MURDER OCCURRED AT 7:00 PM, ON THE EVENING OF WEDNESDAY, FEBRUARY 16, 23 YEARS AGO.

AT THE TIME, SUMI WAS 58 YEARS OLD.

Kawamoto Osteopathy Clinic
SHE HAD GONE ALONE TO VISIT AN INDEPEN-DENTLY RUN MASSAGE CLINIC.
SHE HAD APPARENTLY MADE A PRACTICE OF ATTENDING THIS CLINIC ONCE A MONTH IN COMPLETE PRIVACY FOR A BRIEF RESPITE FROM THE WORKING WORLD.
IN ORDER TO KEEP HER PERSONAL LIFE ENTIRELY SEPARATE FROM HER WORK LIFE, SHE DELIBERATELY REFUSED A COMPANY CHAUFFEUR.
ZSH
THEN, ON HER WAY HOME, SHE WAS ATTACKED.
THIEF!

SOME-BODY, HELP!
THAT MAN!
THE MAN IN THE BLACK COAT! ARREST HIM!
HE WENT TOWARD THE STATION!
THE LOCAL RESIDENTS HEARD THE SHOUTS AND CAME RUNNING,
BUT SUMI WAS ALREADY GONE.

HER BODY WAS STILL WARM, SO THEY KNEW SHE HAD ONLY JUST BEEN KILLED.
SUMI'S CRIES WERE IN VAIN.
OR PERHAPS IT WAS BECAUSE SHE USED THE LAST OF HER STRENGTH FOR THOSE SHOUTS THAT SHE DIED MORE QUICKLY.
SNAP
SHE DIED FROM HYPOVOLEMIC SHOCK AFTER BEING STABBED TWICE NEAR THE HEART.
NO ONE KNOWS WHERE THE KNIFE CAME FROM, AND NO FINGER-PRINTS WERE FOUND ON THE WEAPON.
SUMI WAS IN THE HABIT OF CARRYING A SIGNIFICANT AMOUNT OF CASH.
THERE WAS ALWAYS AT LEAST ONE MILLION YEN IN HER WALLET, BUT ALL THE BILLS HAD BEEN REMOVED.
A MUG-GING GONE WRONG.
AT A GLANCE, THE CASE IS SIMPLE.

A MUGGER TRIED TO TAKE HER MONEY, MET WITH UNEXPECTED RESISTANCE, AND STABBED HER IN THE STRUGGLE.
RUSTLE
Otonashi Family Inheritance RESOURCE FILE
AND THAT IS THE STORY.
BUT WITH NO OTHER CLUES OR WITNESS REPORTS, THE INVESTIGATION QUICKLY RAN INTO A DEAD END.

WHILE HOLDING ON TO THE MUGGING THEORY AS THE MOST LIKELY,
THE POLICE ALSO LOOKED INTO THE POSSIBILITY OF A PREMEDITATED MURDER MADE TO *LOOK* LIKE A MUGGING.

SUMI-SAN HAD MADE A LOT OF ENEMIES AT WORK AS WELL AS AT HOME.

ADDITIONALLY, HER FAMILY, AND KÔYA-SAN, HAD MOTIVE AS WELL.

YES, MOM WOULD CUT TIES WITH ANYONE WHO OPPOSED HER OR DISOBEYED HER.

ALL OF YOU KNEW THAT SUMI-SAN WENT TO THE MASSAGE CLINIC ONCE A MONTH.
YOU COULD HAVE PLANNED TO AMBUSH HER ON HER RETURN.
OF COURSE, EVERYONE IN THE COMPANY'S UPPER ECHELONS KNEW ABOUT THE MASSAGE CLINIC, TOO.
AND ANYONE COULD HAVE DONE SOME RESEARCH AND SET UP AN AMBUSH IF THEY'D WANTED TO.
SHE WAS OPPOSED TO KAORUKO-SAN'S MARRIAGE TO KŌYA-SAN,
AND TO RYŌMA-SAN'S AND SUSUMU-SAN'S INDIVIDUAL CAREER GOALS.
CHAIRMAN OTONASHI SENSED HIS CHILDREN'S UNHAPPINESS AS WELL AS AN IMPENDING CRISIS FOR THE GROUP.
EACH OF THESE FACTORS WAS A REASON FOR WANTING SUMI-SAN OUT OF THE WAY.

MY BROTHER AND I OFTEN FOUND OURSELVES WISHING THAT MOM WASN'T AROUND.
AND I NEVER COULD GET INTO HER GOOD GRACES.

Heh.
SHE EVEN TOLD ME IF I DIDN'T CALL OFF MY RELATIONSHIP WITH KAORUKO, SHE WOULD RUIN MY COMPANY.

BUT IF I DID, SHE WOULD GIVE ME A SUBSTANTIAL SUM OF MONEY IN RETURN.
THAT WOULD MAKE ANYONE FEEL A LITTLE HOMICIDAL.

BUT BECAUSE EACH OF YOU HAD AN ALIBI, YOU WERE ALL REMOVED FROM CONSIDERATION.
AT SEVEN THAT NIGHT, CHAIRMAN OTONASHI WAS IN A DIFFERENT PREFECTURE, IN A MEETING WITH ABOUT A DOZEN WITNESSES.

RYÔMA-SAN AND SUSUMU-SAN WERE BOTH AT THE GROUP'S MAIN OFFICE, OVER AN HOUR'S DRIVE AWAY FROM THE SCENE OF THE CRIME.
AND YOU WERE SEEN INSIDE THE OFFICE RIGHT AROUND SEVEN.

IN PARTICULAR, PEOPLE SAW THE TWO OF YOU FIGHTING IN THE OFFICE, CORRECT?
SFF
I WAS IN MY TWENTIES, AND NII-SAN WAS JUST OVER 30.
WE WERE YOUNG THEN.
CLACK
HE HAD BEEN TRAINING AT A FAMOUS RESTAURANT BEHIND MOM'S BACK.
BUT SHE CAUGHT ON AND MADE SURE HE HAD TO WORK AT THE MAIN OFFICE. THE STRESS WAS GETTING TO HIM.
FOR MY PART, I WAS ON EDGE BECAUSE I WAS ONLY ALLOWED TO WORK AS HIS AS-SISTANT.
SO WHILE HE HATED HIS JOB, I WISHED I COULD HAVE IT.
IT DIDN'T TAKE MUCH TO TO GET US ARGUING.

IN-DEED.
I UNDER-STAND THAT MANY OF YOUR ASSOCIATES WERE AWARE OF THE BAD BLOOD BETWEEN YOU.
BUT YOU HAD NEVER SHOWN SUCH OVERT HOSTILITIES WITHIN COMPANY WALLS BEFORE.
WHICH MADE YOUR ALIBI ALL THE MORE INDISPUT-ABLE.
COINCIDENCE OR NOT, IT HELPED YOUR CASE.
CLENCH
WHIRL
YOU, KÔYA-SAN, WERE OUT MAKING THE ROUNDS, TALKING TO POTENTIAL BUYERS.
AMIDST ALL YOUR NEGOTIA-TIONS, YOU DIDN'T HAVE TIME TO SLIP AWAY AND DO THE DEED.

YOU HADN'T EARNED A NAME FOR YOURSELF YET, AND I HEAR YOU COULD BE RATHER PUSHY?
I WAS 33 AT THE TIME.
I HAD NO CON-NECTIONS—OBVIOUSLY I HAD TO WORK HARD TO GET MY FOOT IN THE DOOR.

FORCING AN INTER-VIEW WAS JUST PART OF THE JOB.
OF COURSE.
AND BECAUSE OF THAT, YOUR ALIBI IS ROCK SOLID.

IF YOU HAD GIVEN UP AFTER THE FIRST "NO THANK YOU," YOU MIGHT HAVE HAD TIME TO MAKE IT TO THE SCENE OF THE CRIME, AFTER ALL.
IT PAYS TO BE A HARD WORKER.

KAORUKO-SAN HAD INJURED HER LEFT LEG.
AND WAS ALONE IN YOUR APARTMENT.
BUT ORIGINALLY, SHE HAD HAD PLANS TO GO OUT TO DINNER WITH A FRIEND THAT DAY.
THEY HAD RESER-VATIONS AND SHOULD HAVE BEEN AT THE RESTAU-RANT BY 6:30.

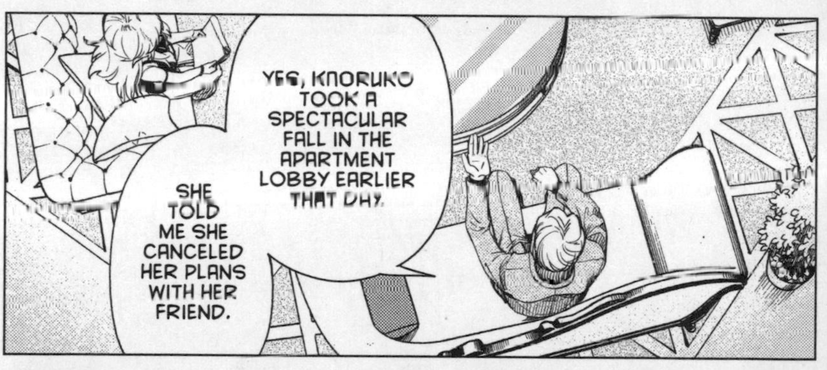
YES, KAORUKO TOOK A SPECTACULAR FALL IN THE APARTMENT LOBBY EARLIER THAT DAY.
SHE TOLD ME SHE CANCELED HER PLANS WITH HER FRIEND.

A NEIGHBOR WAS THERE AND ABLE TO HELP HER—THEY PUT SOME COLD COMPRESSES ON IT, BUT THE SWELLING HAD GOTTEN WORSE IN THE EVENING.
I TOOK HER TO THE HOSPITAL AFTER I GOT HOME FROM WORK LATE THAT NIGHT.
WE FOUND OUT SHE'D BROKEN HER LEFT TIBIA, SO SHE STAYED THE NIGHT THERE.

KAORUKO-SAN HAD HAD PLANS BEFORE, BUT THANKS TO HER LITTLE ACCIDENT, SHE ALMOST LOST HER ALIBI.
NEVER-THELESS, SHE, TOO, NARROWLY ESCAPED SUSPICION.
SHE CERTAINLY COULD NOT HAVE ATTACKED AND KILLED SUMI-SAN ON THAT LEG, AND BECAUSE THE MURDERER WAS BELIEVED TO BE MALE, SHE WAS OUTSIDE OF THE SUSPECT POOL.
HOW VERY FOR-TUNATE FOR HER.
Otonashi Family Inheritance
RESOURCE FILE
FWOOSH
IWA-NAGA-SAN.
WHAT ARE YOU TRYING TO SAY?

ARE YOU TRYING TO PROVE THAT GRANDFATHER SPECIFICALLY HAD GRANDMOTHER KILLED WHEN EVERYONE ELSE HAD AN ALIBI?
EVEN IF THAT'S THE CASE, DO YOU HAVE TO BE SO MALICIOUS ABOUT IT?
IT SOUNDS LIKE...
EXCEPT FOR AUNT KAORUKO, EVERYONE KNEW ABOUT GRANDFATHER'S MURDER PLOT,
AND DELIBERATELY MADE SURE PEOPLE REMEMBERED WHERE THEY WERE AT THE TIME OF THE CRIME.
IS THAT WHAT YOU'RE INSINUATING?

PERISH THE THOUGHT!
I WOULD NEVER DO SOMETHING SO LOW-CLASS.

WHAP
?!

IT'S A LITTLE LATE FOR YOU TO BE TALKING ABOUT CLASS.

I HAVE ACTED WITH NOTHING BUT CLASS THROUGH THE ENTIRE PROCEEDINGS!
YOU GAVE UP ANY ILLUSION OF CLASS WHEN YOU SUGGESTED AN ALLIANCE.

WHAP
EX-CUSE HIM.
I APOLOGIZE FOR MY COMPAN-ION'S BAD MANNERS.
AHEM
IT IS TRUE THAT I SUG-GESTED AN ALLIANCE.
BUT DESPITE ALL YOUR CLAIMS OF SELFLESS-NESS, I DID NOT EXPECT THE MATTER TO BE RESOLVED SO QUICKLY.

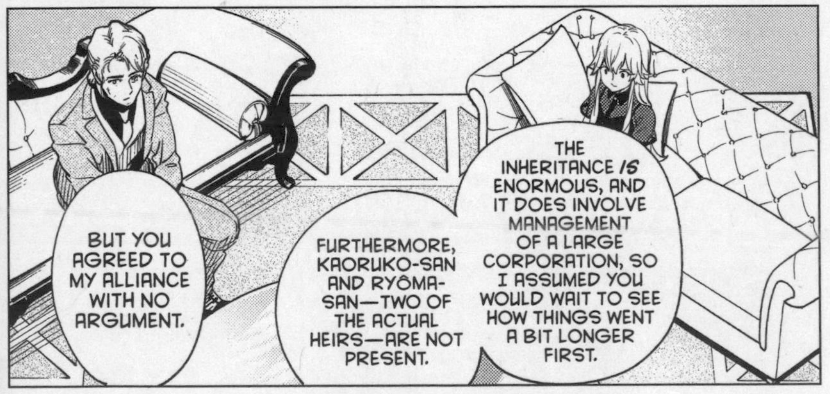
THE INHERITANCE *IS* ENORMOUS, AND IT DOES INVOLVE MANAGEMENT OF A LARGE CORPORATION, SO I ASSUMED YOU WOULD WAIT TO SEE HOW THINGS WENT A BIT LONGER FIRST.
FURTHERMORE, KAORUKO-SAN AND RYÔMA-SAN—TWO OF THE ACTUAL HEIRS—ARE NOT PRESENT.
BUT YOU AGREED TO MY ALLIANCE WITH NO ARGUMENT.

IT'S AS IF YOU WERE ALL TRYING TO SAY YOU WOULD LIKE TO SETTLE THIS QUICKLY AND PEACE-ABLY...
...BE-FORE ANYONE UN-EARTHS YOUR SKEL-ETONS.
THESE ARE THE ACTIONS OF PEOPLE WHO HAVE BIGGER CONCERNS THAN AN INHERITANCE, WOULDN'T YOU AGREE?

ESPECIALLY BECAUSE THIS ALLI- ANCE GOES AGAINST CHAIRMAN OTONASHI'S WISHES.
IF YOU HAD NO SUCH CONCERNS, I BELIEVE YOU WOULD HAVE TAKEN THE ASSIGNMENT MORE SERIOUSLY.
...
PERHAPS IT IS A COINCIDENCE THAT YOU ALL HAVE AN ALIBI.
OR PERHAPS NYOMA SAN, SUSUMU-SAN, KÔYA-SAN, AND CHAIRMAN OTONASHI WERE ALL COMPLICIT,
AND ARRANGED TO HAVE ALIBIS BEFORE- HAND.
BECAUSE KAORUKO- SAN HAD NOT BEEN INFORMED OF THE PLOT,
SHE VERY NEARLY LOST HER ALIBI.
HEE HEE
DON'T YOU THINK IT'S MORE FUN TO INTERPRET IT THAT WAY?

JOLT
I DON'T CARE ABOUT THE INHERITANCE.
AND I KNOW THAT MY UNCLES AND GRANDFATHER WOULDN'T DO ANYTHING TO CHEAT ANYONE OUT OF THEIR FAIR SHARE.
THAT'S WHY I AGREED TO YOUR ALLIANCE—BECAUSE IT WAS BETTER THAN STARTING A FAMILY FEUD.
AND HERE YOU ARE,
MOCKING US BECAUSE IT'S "MORE FUN"?
YOU REALLY DON'T HAVE ANY CLASS!

MAYBE HE KNOWS SOMETHING HE CAN TELL US NOW THAT SO MUCH TIME HAS PASSED. ONLY HE WANTS US TO FIGURE IT OUT.
THMP
...IF THEY WERE ALL IN IT TOGETHER—GRANDFATHER INCLUDED—THEN THERE'D BE NO POINT IN THIS MEETING OR THIS ASSIGN-MENT.
BECAUSE THEN MY UNCLES WOULD KNOW THAT GRANDFATHER DID IT.
INDEED.
I NEVER BELIEVED THAT THEY WERE ACCOM-PLICES, EITHER.
CHAIRMAN OTONASHI DENIES IT, AS WELL.
BUT HE DID SAY...
...WE MUST ALWAYS FACE PUNISHMENT FOR OUR CRIMES.

SO HE WANTS ME TO CONFESS, IS THAT IT?

IS THAT THE POINT OF THIS ASSIGN-MENT?
GRIN
IS IT?
SIMPLY PLANNING TO COMMIT MURDER DOES CONSTITUTE A CRIME.
UNCLE ...?

ALL RIGHT.
I ADMIT IT.
23 YEARS AGO, MY BROTHER AND I DID HAVE A PLAN TO KILL OUR MOTHER.
BUT SOMEONE ELSE KILLED HER BEFORE WE WERE READY.
SO WE NEVER CARRIED IT OUT.
...!

JOLT
YOU AND MY DAD?
BUT YOU'VE HATED EACH OTHER FOR MORE THAN 30 YEARS!
YOU WERE FIGHT-ING ON THE DAY OF THE CRIME!

BUT WHAT IF YOU WERE IN CAHOOTS, AND WERE ONLY PRETENDING TO HAVE A FIGHT?
FOR EXAMPLE, LET'S SAY THE TWO OF YOU WENT INTO AN EMPTY MEETING ROOM AND START ARGUING.
THE PEOPLE OUTSIDE HEARD THE VOICES AND SOUNDS OF AN ALTER-CATION.

BUT ONE OF THE VOICES WAS PRE-RECORDED.
ONLY ONE OF YOU WAS IN THE ROOM, ACTING OUT A VICIOUS FIGHT.

PEOPLE WOULD THINK THAT YOU WERE BOTH INSIDE THE ROOM.
MEANWHILE, THE OTHER ONE OF YOU WENT OUT TO COMMIT MURDER.

THAT'S RIGHT.
THAT WAS OUR PLAN FOR CREATING AN ALIBI.
WE WERE BOTH MISERABLE IN THOSE DAYS.
BUT THEN MY BROTHER CAME TO ME WITH A PLAN.
KA-CHAK
WHAT'S SO IMPORTANT YOU NEEDED TO SEE ME ABOUT?
NII-SAN.

I FIGURED YOU WERE THE ONLY ONE I COULD ASK.
THE WAY THINGS ARE, OUR FUTURES—
AND THE GROUP'S FUTURE—ARE DOOMED.

SO I'M GOING TO KILL MOM.

I JUST NEED YOU TO HELP ME CREATE AN ALIBI.
I'LL DO THE DIRTY WORK.

I SEE...

NII-SAN WAS GOING TO DO THIS WHETHER I AGREED TO HELP OR NOT.
コツ
CLACK
コツ
CLACK
AND I KNEW JUST AS WELL AS HE DID THAT MOM'S EXISTENCE WAS ENDANGERING EVERYTHING AROUND HER.

IF I BACKED DOWN, I WOULD BE INFERIOR TO HIM THE REST OF MY LIFE.
もぐ
MUNCH

I ASSUME YOU HAVE A PLAN.

AND I ADMIT I WAS TICKLED TO THINK THAT HE NEEDED ME, AND THAT HE TRUSTED ME TO BE HIS ACCOMPLICE.
BUT SINCE I NEVER COULD OFFER TO DO THE DEED MYSELF,
I'LL STILL ALWAYS BE LESS THAN HIM.
OUR PLAN WAS ROUGHLY THE SAME AS YOU DESCRIBED.
BUT WE NEEDED TO LAY MORE GROUND-WORK TO DIVERT SUSPICION.
KAPOW

WHAK
KAPOW
BONK
Don't hit my glasses!
You punch like a T-rex!
HUH? WHAT THE—?
A FIGHT?
CRASH
I NOTICED THEY WERE GETTING EVEN WORSE, BUT...
SOMEBODY SHOULD PROBABLY STOP THEM.
WHAM
"THERE'S NOTHING UNUSUAL ABOUT THE TWO OF THEM ARGUING AND HITTING EACH OTHER IN THE OFFICE."
"YES, I KNOW THEY'RE DUKING IT OUT IN AN EMPTY MEETING ROOM, BUT IT'S SAFER TO JUST STAY OUT OF IT."
THAT'S THE ATMOSPHERE WE WERE HOPING TO CREATE.
GENERAL MANAGER OTO-NASHI!
I HAVE BAD NEWS!

THAT WAS THE DAY MOM WAS KILLED...
IT'S PRESIDENT OTONASHI ...!
...AND THAT FIGHT BECAME OUR ALIBI FOR FEBRUARY 16, 23 YEARS AGO.
WHO KILLED MOM?
WE HAD PLANNED TO MURDER OUR MOTHER AFTER HER VISIT TO THE MASSAGE CLINIC THE NEXT MONTH.
WHAM
I...

I DIDN'T WANT TO BE SAVED BY LUCK! THIS ISN'T WHAT I WANTED!

DID YOU EVER SUSPECT THAT MAYBE CHAIRMAN OTONASHI HAD DONE IT?

YES. BUT DAD HAD AN ALIBI.
AND THERE WAS NO INDICATION THAT HE HAD HIRED SOMEONE TO DO IT.
THAT'S WHY THE POLICE DECIDED MOM'S DEATH WAS A MUGGING GONE WRONG.

BUT NOW DAD'S GIVEN US THIS AS-SIGNMENT.
IF HE DIDN'T KILL HER, OF COURSE I'M GOING TO THINK HE'S TRYING TO GET ME AND MY BROTHER TO CONFESS,
AND MAKE US PAY FOR PLOTTING TO KILL OUR MOTHER.

...AND I SUSPECT NII-SAN HAD THE SAME FEELING.
WE NEVER ACTED ON IT, BUT WE DID PLAN A MURDER. THAT GUILT IS A HEAVY BURDEN TO BEAR FOR YOUR WHOLE LIFE.
MAYBE HE SENT RION HERE...
...BECAUSE HE WANTED HIS DAUGHTER TO LEARN OF THAT GUILT, AS SOME FORM OF PENANCE.
GASP
WAIT... UNCLE. IS THAT WHY YOU AND DAD HAVE BEEN FIGHTING FOR THE LAST 23 YEARS?
TO ERASE ANY CHANCE THAT ANYONE WOULD SUSPECT YOU OF WORKING TOGETHER TO COMMIT A CRIME?
DON'T GET ANY FUNNY IDEAS.
I DO HATE MY BROTHER.

MANAGEMENT OF THIS COMPANY IS, TO ME, THE MOST IMPORTANT THING IN THE WORLD, AND HE JUST THREW IT ALL AWAY.
HE'S HAPPY TO GO HIS OWN WAY, EVERYONE ELSE BE DAMNED.
AND DESPITE THAT, WHEN HE *WAS* RUNNING THE GROUP, HE WAS BETTER AT IT THAN I WAS.

EVEN HIS OWN TALENT MEANT NOTHING TO HIM— HE JUST TOSSED IT ASIDE.

NEVER MIND THE FACT THAT I WISHED I COULD HAVE IT.
Please don't quit!

IF NII-SAN HAD STAYED IN THE GROUP, HE WOULD HAVE BEEN MADE ITS PRESIDENT LONG AGO.

I'VE ALWAYS FELT INFERIOR TO HIM.

WHAT A DESPICABLE MAN.
HE'S BETTER THAN YOU.
THMP
Hmph.
MM-HM.

BUT I DO FEEL A LITTLE BETTER.
SO I CAN AT LEAST THANK YOU FOR GIVING ME THE OPPORTUNI-TY TO COME FORWARD.
NO, MAYBE I SHOULD BE THINKING DAD. YOU'RE JUST THE JUDGE, AFTER ALL.

BOW

THEN WHAT ABOUT KÔYA-SAN AND KAORUKO-SAN?

WERE YOU NOT PLANNING TO MURDER SUMI OTONASHI-SAN 23 YEARS AGO?

THE TIMING OF KAORUKO-SAN BREAKING HER LEG IS TOO PERFECT.
SO I THOUGHT, WHAT IF SHE TRIED TO CREATE AN ALIBI THUS...

ON THE AFTERNOON OF THE MURDER, KAORUKO-SAN WOULD DELIBERATELY FALL IN A PLACE WHERE THERE WERE PEOPLE TO SEE HER,
AND PRETEND TO HAVE BADLY INJURED HER LEG.
AT THAT POINT, NOTHING WOULD HAVE BEEN BROKEN.

IN THE EVENING, SHE WOULD SNEAK OUT OF THE APART-MENT,

KILL SUMI-SAN, AND MAKE IT LOOK LIKE A MUGGING GONE WRONG.

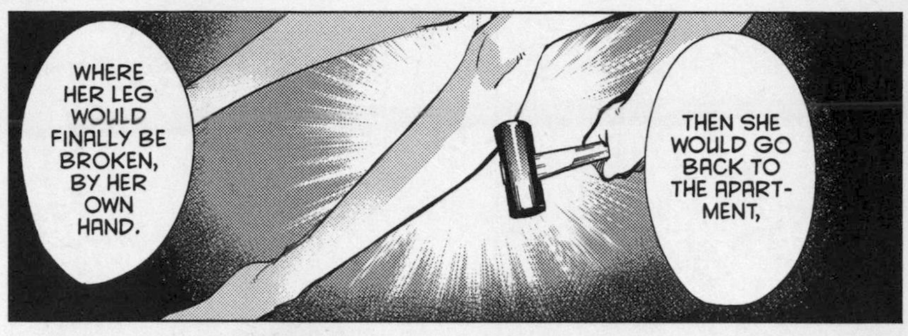
THEN SHE WOULD GO BACK TO THE APART-MENT,
WHERE HER LEG WOULD FINALLY BE BROKEN, BY HER OWN HAND.

THAT WAY, EVERYONE WOULD THINK THAT THE LEG HAD BEEN BROKEN IN THE AFTER-NOON,
AND BELIEVE SHE COULD NOT HAVE COMMITTED THE CRIME.
IT WOULD TAKE A LOT OF COMMITMENT, BUT IT'S NOT IMPOSSIBLE.
MAYBE YOU HELPED HER ONCE YOU GOT HOME

HOW DO YOU COME UP WITH THESE THINGS? IT MAKES MY LEG HURT JUST THINKING ABOUT IT.

A WOMAN WOULDN'T MISTAKE HER OWN DAUGHTER FOR A MAN, EVEN IF HER FACE WAS HIDDEN.
WE KNOW THE KILLER WAS A MAN BECAUSE OF *SUMI*-SAN'S LAST WORDS.

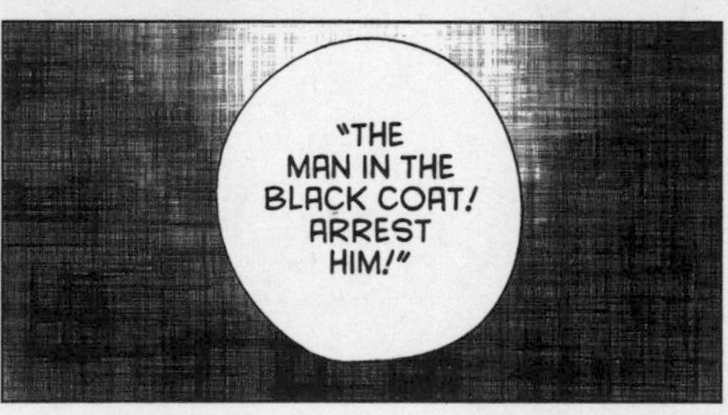
"THE MAN IN THE BLACK COAT! ARREST HIM!"

BUT DID THOSE LAST WORDS REALLY COME FROM SUMI-SAN?
THE LOCAL RESIDENTS WHO HEARD IT LIKELY DIDN'T KNOW HER REAL VOICE.
PERHAPS KAORUKO-SAN PRETENDED TO BE SUMI-SAN.
AND SHE SHOUTED FROM BESIDE THE BODY SO PEOPLE WOULD HEAR HER AND *THINK* THE KILLER WAS MALE.

IT WOULD BE TOO RISKY.
IF THE RESIDENTS CAME OUT TOO SOON, THEY WOULD FIND KAORUKO.
AND IT'S VERY LIKELY THEY WOULD HAVE SEEN HER RUNNING AWAY.

SUMI-SAN CRIED OUT AFTER THE KILLER GOT AWAY.
THAT'S WHY THE RESIDENTS NEVER LAID EYES ON THE MURDERER.
かた
CLACK
BESIDES, IF A MURDER PLOT INVOLVES KILLING SOMEONE IN A RESIDENTIAL AREA, THE PERPETRATOR WOULD COVER THE VICTIM'S MOUTH AT THE TIME OF THE SLAYING,
MAKING SURE THEY COULDN'T USE THEIR VOICE.
QUITE SO.

FURTHER-MORE, IF THEY LEFT ANY CLUES POINTING TO THEM-SELF,
OR IF THE RESIDENTS FOUND SUMI-SAN IN TIME TO GET HER HELP, THEN THE WHOLE PLAN WOULD BE RUINED.
THEY WOULDN'T LEAVE THE VICTIM'S SIDE UNTIL THEY WERE SURE SHE WAS DEAD.

IT WAS AN UNPLANNED MURDER COMMITTED BY A MUGGER WHO HAD NEVER SEEN SUMI-SAN BEFORE.
THAT IS THE ONLY PLAUSIBLE REASON THAT SUMI-SAN WOULD HAVE HAD ENOUGH ENERGY TO SCREAM AFTER THE KILLER HAD LEFT THE SCENE.

BUT YOU WON'T GET A BETTER OPPORTUNITY.
TMP
AND IF YOU ASK SUSUMU-SAN, IT WILL HELP YOU FEEL BETTER.
FINE. I'LL CONFESS.
YOU HAVE IT BACK-WARDS.

KAORUKO'S BROKEN LEG WASN'T WHAT MADE IT POSSIBLE FOR HER TO COMMIT THE CRIME.
IT WAS THE BROKEN LEG THAT THREW A WRENCH IN OUR PLANS.
KAORUKO AND I PLOTTED TO KILL HER, TOO.
AND, LIKE SUSUMU-SAN AND RYÔMA-SAN, WE WERE WAIT-ING FOR HER TO BE ON HER WAY HOME FROM THE MASSAGE CLINIC.
B-DMP
I DOUBT IT WAS A COINCI-DENCE.
WE WERE GOING TO DO IT THAT VERY DAY.
IT'S PROBABLY JUST BECAUSE THAT'S THE ONLY TIME WE COULD BE SURE SHE WAS ON THE MOVE AND ALONE.
AND WE PLANNED TO FALSIFY THE TIME OF HER INJURY, JUST LIKE YOU EXPLAINED.

I CAN'T TAKE IT ANYMORE.

IF WE DON'T DO SOMETHING, SHE'LL TEAR US APART.
AND SHE'LL RUIN YOUR BUSINESS.

BUT THIS PLAN WILL WORK.
I'VE BEEN A SPOILED RICH GIRL MY WHOLE LIFE. NO ONE WOULD EVER SUSPECT I WOULD BREAK MY OWN LEG.

ON THE DAY OF THE MURDER, AS PER KAORUKO'S PLAN, I WAS RUNNING AROUND ON BUSINESS ALL DAY, GIVING MYSELF AN ALIBI.
WHEN NIGHT FELL, I WENT BACK TO THE APART-MENT...

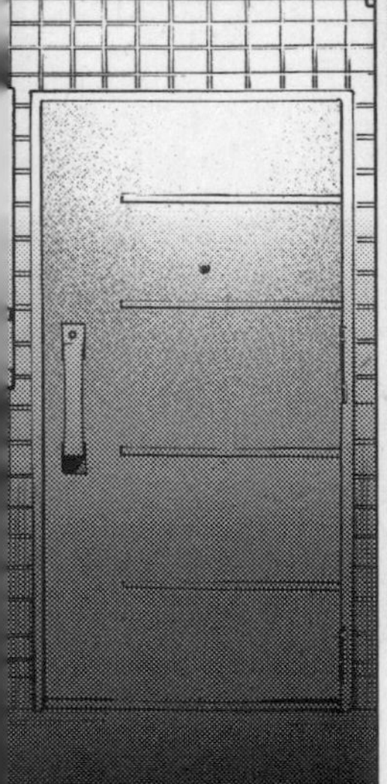

...EXPECTING KAORUKO TO HAVE ALREADY COMMITTED THE MURDER.

KA-CHAK

KAORU-KO?

PAH

KÔYA-SAN, I'M SO SORRY.

I... I MESSED UP.

KAORU-KO.
I THINK I REALLY DID BREAK MY LEG WHEN I FELL EARLIER.
DASH
THROB
THROB
HOW COULD I BE SO STUPID!
EVEN IF I DID MANAGE TO AMBUSH HER,
I COULDN'T HAVE RUN AWAY LIKE THIS...
I JUST DIDN'T THINK I COULD DO IT AND STILL GET AWAY.
YEAH.
THAT LOOKS BAD. IT MUST REALLY HURT.
YOU SHOULD HAVE GONE STRAIGHT TO THE HOSPITAL.

I COULDN'T LEAVE THE APARTMENT WITHOUT LETTING YOU KNOW WHAT HAPPENED.
LET'S JUST GET YOU TO A DOCTOR.

I'M SORRY.

IT WAS AT THE HOSPITAL THAT WE GOT THE NEWS OF HER DEATH.

KAORUKO AND I WERE BOTH STUNNED.
SOME-ONE SOME-WHERE HAD KILLED HER.
AND ON THE VERY DAY AN UNFORESEEN ACCIDENT HAD PUT AN END TO OUR PLANS TO DO JUST THAT.
IT WAS A LITTLE TOO CREEPY FOR DIVINE PROVI-DENCE.

OF COURSE WE HAD OUR SUSPICIONS ABOUT CHAIRMAN OTONASHI.
MAYBE HE WAS ON TO OUR PLANS AND DECIDED TO ACT FIRST.
IN ANY CASE, WE WERE GLAD IT ALL WORKED OUT, SO WE DECIDED TO FORGET IT AND MOVE ON WITH OUR LIVES.

AND THEN WE GOT THIS ASSIGN-MENT.
EVEN IF HE *IS* THE KILLER, I CAN'T BELIEVE HIS ONLY GOAL IS TO CONFESS HIS OWN GUILT.

I SENSED THAT THIS WAS SOME ROUNDABOUT WAY OF HIS TO GET US TO CONFESS *OUR* CRIMES.
KAORU-KO'S BEEN SCARED OUT OF HER MIND, TOO.
THAT'S WHY *I'M* HERE. IT WAS OUR ONLY OPTION.

SIGH...
GSH

BUT IT NEVER OCCURRED TO ME THAT RYÔMA-SAN AND SUSUMU-SAN HAD PLOTTED HER DEATH, TOO.
IT'S SUCH A LOAD OFF MY MIND, I FEEL LIKE IT'S MORE THAN I DESERVE.

AND I'M SURE KAORUKO WILL FEEL A LOT BETTER, TOO.
MAYBE THE CHAIRMAN IS JUST TRYING TO SETTLE HIS PAST ACCOUNTS, BECAUSE HE DOESN'T THINK HE HAS MUCH TIME LEFT.
MAYBE THAT'S WHY HE WANTED US TO GET OUR GUILT OUT INTO THE OPEN, TOO—
TO FREE US FROM THE WEIGHT OF IT ALL.

SIGH...
WELL, LITTLE MISS IWA-NAGA?
THE HEIRS' CRIMES HAVE ALL BEEN EXPOSED, JUST LIKE YOU WANTED.
NOW CAN WE END THIS FARCE?

OH, THIS ISN'T OVER.
IT DOESN'T MATTER TO ME WHAT ANY OF YOU WERE DOING AT THE TIME—I'M NOT HERE TO MAKE ACCUSATIONS OR HEAR APOLOGIES.
THE STATUTE OF LIMITATIONS IS LONG PAST, AND THAT IS NOT THE MATTER AT HAND.
HOW DID CHAIRMAN OTONASHI KILL SUMI OTONASHI-SAN?
THAT IS THE ONLY ANSWER I AM LOOKING FOR.
YOUR CRIMES ARE UNIMPORTANT.

THEN WHY DID YOU MAKE US ADMIT TO PLOTTING TO KILL OUR MOTHER?!
YOU'VE BOTH BEEN SO FOCUSED ON MAKING SURE NO ONE FOUND OUT ABOUT YOUR CRIMES,
I PRESUME NEITHER OF YOU IS PREPARED TO ANSWER THE ACTUAL QUESTION.
I'M SURE RION-SAN HAS HAD A TERRIBLE TIME CONCENTRATING IN THIS ATMO-SPHERE, AS OBVIOUS AS IT WAS THAT PEOPLE WERE HIDING THINGS.
SO I FIGURED WE WOULD NEVER GET ANYWHERE IF WE DIDN'T GET THAT OUT OF THE WAY FIRST.
I HAVE BEEN TRUSTED WITH THE ROLE OF JUDGE, AND I MUST PERFORM MY DUTIES WITH PRECISION.
CHAIRMAN OTONASHI'S PAST SUCCESS WAS BUILT ON THE DEATH OF ANOTHER. HE WISHES TO RIGHT THE WRONG OF THAT PAST.
TUG
SUCCESS CAN, AT TIMES, BE HARMFUL. IT CAN EVEN LEAD TO SELF-DESTRUC-TION.
THAT IS WHY WE MUST CORRECT THE PAST.

NOW THEN.
HOW DID CHAIRMAN OTONASHI KILL HIS WIFE?
THERE IS AN ANSWER.
THINK CARE-FULLY.

~Scene from the novel that was omitted for space reasons~
Well said!
Praise from you doesn't mean much...

YOUR CRIMES ARE UNIM-PORTANT.

HOW DID CHAIRMAN OTONASHI KILL HIS WIFE?

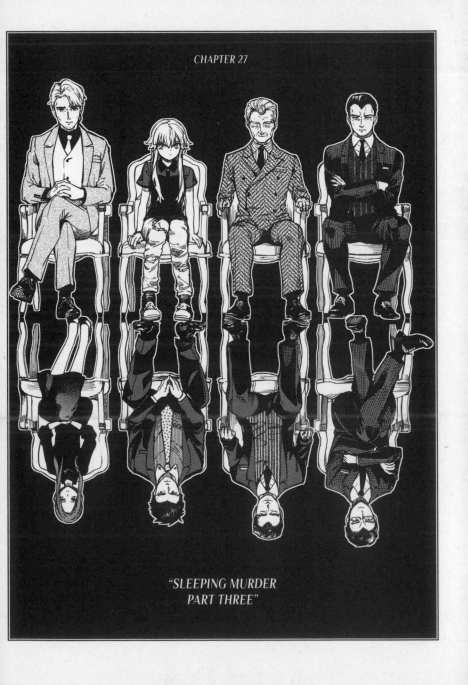

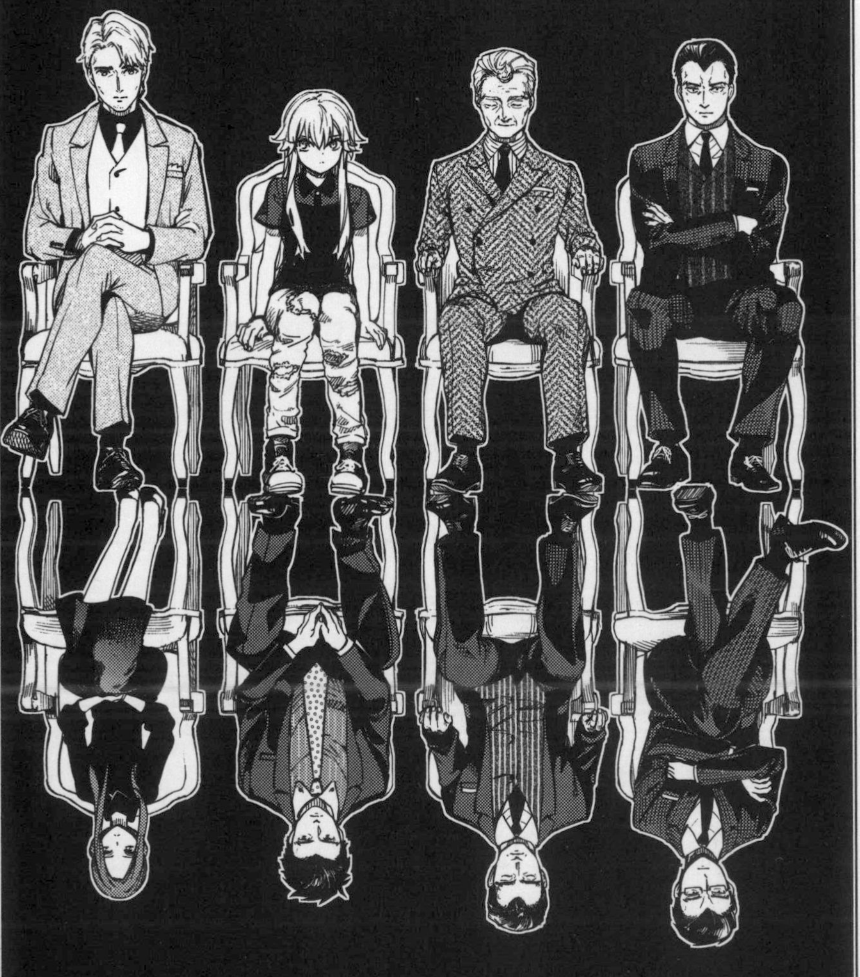
CHAPTER 27
"SLEEPING MURDER
PART THREE"

G-GNN
I'M GOING TO STEP OUTSIDE FOR A MINUTE.

I SHOULD AT LEAST TELL KAORUKO WHAT'S HAPPENED.

I'M GOING TO GET SOME FRESH AIR, TOO.

GLARE

バタン
SHUT
BEEP
ボフ
BOFF

WHEW...
!
WHUMP
ARE YOU EMOTIONALLY FATIGUED, PERHAPS?
SHALL WE RETURN TO OUR ROOM AS WELL?
NO, THAT'S OKAY.
I HAVE NO IDEA WHAT YOU'D DO TO ME ONCE WE GOT THERE.
WE **WILL** BE SPENDING THE NIGHT TOGETHER!
THIS LOOK REALLY SUITS YOU, KURÔ-SENPAI.

WHY DON'T WE MAKE THESE INTO PAJAMAS?
GSH
THEY WOULDN'T BE COM-FORTABLE TO SLEEP IN.

...DOES CHAIRMAN OTONASHI KNOW THAT HIS CHILDREN WERE ALL PLOTTING TO MURDER HIS WIFE?
NO.
I JUST PRESSED THEM WITH SOME OF MY OWN INFORMATION AND SPECULATION, AND THEY SANG LIKE CANARIES, THAT'S ALL.
I DOUBT THE CHAIRMAN WOULD HAVE CONSIDERED THE POSSIBILITY.

THEN WAS IT EVEN NECESSARY FOR YOU TO BRING IT UP AT ALL?
CHAIRMAN OTONASHI WILL HAVE A HEART ATTACK WHEN HE FINDS OUT.
WHEN YOU MAKE WEIRD ASSIGN-MENTS, YOU GET WEIRD RESULTS.
ROLL
WELL.
MAYBE I'LL BREAK IT TO HIM MYSELF BEFORE THE DAY IS OUT.

AND AS I EXPLAINED EARLIER,
IF THESE THINGS AREN'T OUT IN THE OPEN, THEY'LL ALL BE DISTRACTED BY THEIR SUPERFLUOUS THOUGHTS.
AND IT MADE IT EASIER FOR ME TO LEAD THEM TO THE "ACCURATE FALSE EXPLANATION" THAT I HAVE PREPARED FOR THEM.
YOU'RE NOT GOING TO WAIT FOR THEM TO COME UP WITH THEIR OWN SOLUTIONS?
IT'S EASIER THIS WAY.
I'VE PLANTED ENOUGH HINTS TO GET THEM TO IMAGINE MY ANSWER.
I JUST NEED TO INSINUATE A LITTLE BIT MORE ABOUT THE VICTIM'S MENTALITY AT THE TIME, AND IT WILL BE PERFECT.
BUT I MAY NOT NEED TO BEFORE THEY FIGURE IT OUT ANYWAY.

RION-SAN SHOWS THE MOST PROMISE.
SHE MAY EVEN REACH THE ANSWER I'M LOOKING FOR TONIGHT.

I WAS PREPARED TO LET YOU FIND OUT WHAT SUSUMU AND I DID.
BUT I CAN'T BELIEVE IT DIDN'T END THERE.

I MEAN,
I DIDN'T EXPECT THAT FROM KAORUKO AND KÔYA-SAN.
I DON'T CARE WHAT YOU "EX-PECTED."
IF YOU KNEW I WAS GOING TO FIND OUT, YOU COULD
YOURSELF.
...I'M SORRY.
I WASN'T SURE WHAT I WANTED.
I THOUGHT I WOULD HAVE TO TAKE THAT SECRET TO THE GRAVE.
BUT I ALSO THOUGHT MAYBE I WOULD FEEL BETTER IF YOU OR DAD FOUND OUT.

SO I WAS OKAY WITH THE IDEA OF YOU DISCOVERING THE TRUTH, OR OF DAD ACCUSING ME.
I JUST DIDN'T WANT TO HAVE TO TELL YOU MYSELF.
...OH.
OKAY.
WHEN UNCLE SUSUMU CONFESSED, IT WAS LIKE KOTOKO IWANAGA HAD FORCED HIM INTO IT.
I UNDER-STAND HOW YOU FELT. I'M NOT MAD.

YOU'RE TAKING THIS AWFULLY WELL FOR SOMEONE WHO JUST FOUND OUT THAT HER FATHER TRIED TO KILL HER GRANDMOTHER.

I JUST CAN'T REALLY IMAGINE WHAT KIND OF A PERSON SHE WAS.

SO I GUESS IT JUST DOESN'T REALLY FEEL REAL. . .
I HEARD THAT SHE WAS AN AMAZING WOMAN, AND SHE MADE THE OTONASHI GROUP WHAT IT IS TODAY.
BUT I ALSO GET THAT SHE WAS SO PROB-LEMATIC, HER OWN FAMILY PLOTTED TO KILL HER.
AND YET, WHEN YOU, OR UNCLE SUSUMU, OR UNCLE KÔYA, OR GRAND-FATHER TALK ABOUT HER,
FOR SOME REASON, IT NEVER SOUNDS LIKE YOU HATE HER.

IT'S LIKE, YOU ALL WANTED TO KILL HER, BUT WHATEVER NEGATIVE FEELINGS YOU HAVE ABOUT HER ARE PRETTY WEAK.
SO PART OF ME THINKS THAT THE PAST THAT I'VE HEARD ABOUT ISN'T THE WHOLE TRUTH.
I GET IT.
THERE WAS DEFINITELY HATE BACK THEN.
SHE WAS A TYRANT WHO DIDN'T CONSIDER THE WISHES OR HAPPINESS OF HER CHILDREN, OR EVEN THE FUTURE OF HER COMPANY,
AND WAS A SELFISH MOTHER WITH TERRIBLE JUDGMENT AND NO SELF-CONTROL. THAT'S HOW I SAW HER.
IF SOMEONE DOESN'T GET RID OF HER, SHE'LL RUIN EVERYTHING.

EVERY-ONE SAID SO.
BUT IT'S BEEN A LONG TIME SINCE SHE PASSED AWAY, AND I FINALLY UNDERSTAND.
SHE WASN'T JUST A TYRANT WHO REFUSED TO LISTEN TO ANYONE ELSE.
AND SHE HAD THOUGHT ABOUT OUR HAPPI-NESS.
BUT SHE WAS A VICTIM, TOO.
ORDERED TO DO?
SHE BELIEVED IN THE THINGS SHE WAS ORDERED TO DO, AND SHE WAS GOING TO KEEP DOING THOSE THINGS—THAT'S ALL IT WAS.
BY WHOM?

HER FATHER, DENJIRÔ.

IT WAS MOM WHO EXPANDED THE OTONASHI GROUP TO WHERE IT IS.

BUT SHE DID IT UNDER DENJIRÔ'S ORDERS. HE LAID OUT DETAILED PLANS AND POLICIES WHILE HE WAS STILL ALIVE, AND LEFT THEM TO HER.

THE FIGURE SUMI OTONASHI MERELY OBEYED HIS WISHES AND WENT FORWARD WITH HIS PLANS.

EVEN HER MARRIAGE TO YOUR GRANDFATHER GÔICHI—THAT WAS HIS DECISION, AND SHE DIDN'T GET A SAY IN THE MATTER.

SHE WOULD NEED A FEW CHILDREN TO TAKE OVER THE COMPANY, AND SHE DID EVERYTHING HE WOULD HAVE WANTED...

...WHEN DECIDING HOW TO PASS THE CORPORATION ON TO THOSE CHILDREN, AND WHAT KINDS OF MARRIAGE PARTNERS TO CHOOSE FOR THEM.

THAT'S JUST HOW DETAILED DENJIRÔ'S PLANS WERE FOR HER.
THAT'S WHY SHE TOLD ME—THE ELDEST SON—TO TAKE OVER THE COMPANY, AND ORDERED SUSUMU TO DEVOTE HIMSELF TO ASSISTING ME.
IT'S WHY SHE BELIEVED KAORUKO HAD TO MARRY A MAN WITH A GOOD PEDIGREE, AND WHY SHE TRIED TO GET KÔYA-SAN TO LEAVE HER.
...
IN HER MIND, *THAT* IS WHAT WOULD BRING US THE MOST HAPPINESS.
AND WHAT WAS BEST FOR THE FUTURE OF THE OTONASHI GROUP.
THE SCARY THING ABOUT ALL OF THIS...
...IS THAT FOLLOW-ING THOSE PLANS IS HOW EVERY-THING IN HER LIFE WENT SO WELL.

THE GROUP WAS TRAVELING SMOOTHLY DOWN THE ROAD TO EXPANSION, EXACTLY AS DENJIRÔ HAD PLANNED BEFORE HE DIED.
THE HUSBAND HE HAD CHOSEN FOR HER WAS VERY CAPABLE AND HE PERFORMED HIS DUTIES AS ASSISTANT PERFECTLY.
AND SUSUMU, KAORUKO, AND I WERE RAISED TO BE EXACTLY THE CHILDREN SHE HAD HOPED FOR.
SHE FOLLOWED DENJIRÔ'S INSTRUC-TIONS AND GOT RID OF ANYONE WHO PRO-TESTED.
AND THAT SUCCESS CONTIN-UED FOR DECADES.
AFTER ALL THAT, DO YOU THINK SHE COULD JUST CHANGE COURSE?
COULD SHE, OF HER OWN WILL, DECIDE IT WAS A MISTAKE AND TURN AWAY FROM THAT PLAN?
EVEN THOUGH THERE HADN'T BEEN ANY OBVIOUS SETBACKS OR FAILURES YET?

WELL...
IT WOULD TAKE AN AWFUL LOT OF COURAGE.
IT MIGHT MEAN REJECTING EVERYTHING VALUED HER WHOLE LIFE.
RIGHT.
SHE WAS DENJIRÔ'S PUPPET.
I SUSPECT SHE *DID* REALIZE THAT THE GROUP WAS IN TROUBLE.
AND I'M SURE SHE UNDERSTOOD THAT HER CHILDREN EACH HAD THEIR OWN IDEAS OF HAPPINESS.
BUT ADMITTING THAT AND CHANGING COURSE WOULD MEAN DEFYING DENJIRÔ.
IT WOULD MEAN ABANDONING THE LAWS ON WHICH SHE'D BUILT HER SUCCESS.
BUT SHE COULDN'T ABANDON THEM, ***BECAUSE*** SHE HAD HAD SO MUCH SUCCESS.
YES. SO I SAY SHE...
I SAY ***MOM*** DIED AT A GOOD TIME.

BECAUSE SHE PASSED WHEN SHE DID, SHE NEVER HAD TO SEE THE GROUP FALL APART, OR HER CHILDREN MISERABLE, AND KNOW IT WAS ALL HER FAULT.

SHE NEVER HAD TO COME TO GRIPS WITH THE IDEA THAT SHE HAD BEEN UTTERLY BETRAYED BY EVERYTHING SHE BELIEVED IN.
AND FOR THAT, SHE WAS LUCKY.

I CAN'T BELIEVE YOU ASKED UNCLE SUSUMU FOR HELP.
BUT YOU COULDN'T HAVE PULLED IT OFF BY YOUR-SELF.

I WAS ONLY THINKING OF MY OWN FUTURE.
BUT THAT DOESN'T MEAN I'M TRYING TO JUSTIFY MY VERY REAL PLOT TO KILL HER.

WHEN I GET GOING ON SOMETHING, I LOSE SIGHT OF EVERYTHING ELSE.

SUSUMU, ON THE OTHER HAND, IS ALWAYS CALM AND COLLECTED—HE CAN SEE THE BIG PICTURE. I TRUSTED HIS VIEWS MORE THAN ANYONE ELSE'S.

I WASN'T CUT OUT FOR MANAGING A CORPORATION.

IF I HAD TAKEN OVER THE GROUP, IT PROBABLY WOULD HAVE ENDED UP IN SHAMBLES.

YOU KNOW,
YOU SHOULD TELL UNCLE SUSUMU THAT.
I'VE TOLD HIM A MILLION TIMES. BUT HE WON'T BELIEVE ME.

ALL OF YOU MANAGED TO FIGHT AGAINST THAT CONTROL.
MAYBE THAT'S BECAUSE
...

MAYBE.

IF WE HAD FELT TRULY SUCCESSFUL AFTER FOLLOWING HER ORDERS,

WE MIGHT HAVE ENDED UP AS MORE OF DENJIRÔ'S PUPPETS.

"SUCCESS CAN, AT TIMES, BE HARMFUL.

IT CAN EVEN LEAD TO SELF-DESTRUCTION."

I WONDER IF SHE WAS ACTUALLY GIVING US HINTS THIS WHOLE TIME.

EVERY-ONE HAD AN ALIBI AND A MURDER PLOT.
IF THEY'D PLANNED THE KILLING, THEY WOULDN'T HAVE GIVEN THE VICTIM A CHANCE TO SCREAM.
EVERY FACT IS FULL OF CONTRA-DICTIONS,
AND SERVES TO REMOVE SOMEONE FROM SUSPICION.
BUT IF THIS THEORY IS CORRECT...
DAD, WHAT YOU SAID JUST NOW...
...THAT GRAND-MOTHER DIED AT A GOOD TIME...
I DID SAY THAT. WHAT ABOUT IT?
I...
I THINK I FIGURED OUT WHAT REALLY HAPPENED.

TICK
TICK
I THINK I FIGURED OUT WHAT REALLY HAPPENED ...
...WHEN GRAND-MOTHER WAS KILLED 23 YEARS AGO.
I FEEL NO SENSE OF TRIUMPH ABOUT THE ANSWER I'VE FOUND.

FROM THE VERY BEGIN-NING,

I WAS ONLY GOING WHERE KOTOKO IWANAGA LED ME.

GRAND-MOTHER MURDERED HERSELF.
THAT'S WHY EVERYONE HAD AN ALIBI, INCLUDING GRAND-FATHER.
RION!
MOM WAS THE LAST PERSON WHO WOULD EVER KILL HER-SELF.
SHE HAD COMPLETE CONTROL OVER EVERYTHING AROUND HER.
SHE HAD NO MOTIVE FOR SUICIDE!

BUT PEOPLE WERE PREDICTING THE DOWN-FALL OF THE COMPANY, RIGHT?
ISN'T THAT WHY ALL OF YOU WERE PLOTTING TO KILL HER?
BESIDES, UNCLE SUSUMU, UNCLE KOYA...
YOU MUST HAVE REALIZED THAT GRAND-MOTHER WAS TRAPPED BY HER OWN SUCCESS,
AND THAT IT WAS TOO LATE FOR HER TO STOP AND CHANGE COURSE.
YES. WE'RE OLDER NOW, AND WE CAN SEE THINGS FROM A NEW PERSPECTIVE.
THAT'S WHY *NOW* I BEAR MOM NO ILL WILL, AND I KNOW THAT SHE WAS A VICTIM, TOO.
SHE HAD PLENTY OF MOTIVE TO KILL HERSELF.

GRAND-MOTHER WAS A VERY SAVVY BUSINESS-WOMAN.
SHE MUST HAVE KNOWN THAT, IF SHE HAD KEPT DOING EVERYTHING DENJIRÔ'S WAY, THE COMPANY WOULD BE DOOMED.
BUT IF SHE LET THE GROUP FAIL, SHE WOULD HAVE BEEN BETRAYING DENJIRÔ'S WISHES.
SHE HAD TO AVOID THAT AT ALL COSTS.
BUT **NOT** FOLLOWING HIS ORDERS WOULD BETRAY DENJIRÔ, TOO.
GRAND-MOTHER MUST HAVE BEEN SCARED OUT OF HER MIND.
BECAUSE FOLLOWING THOSE ORDERS HAD BROUGHT HER SO MUCH SUCCESS, DISOBEYING THEM WAS PSYCHO-LOGICALLY IMPOSSIBLE.

THE SOLUTION TO HER PARADOX WAS SUICIDE.

IT WAS THE ONLY WAY TO ESCAPE HER FEARS AND PROTECT THE OTONASHI GROUP.

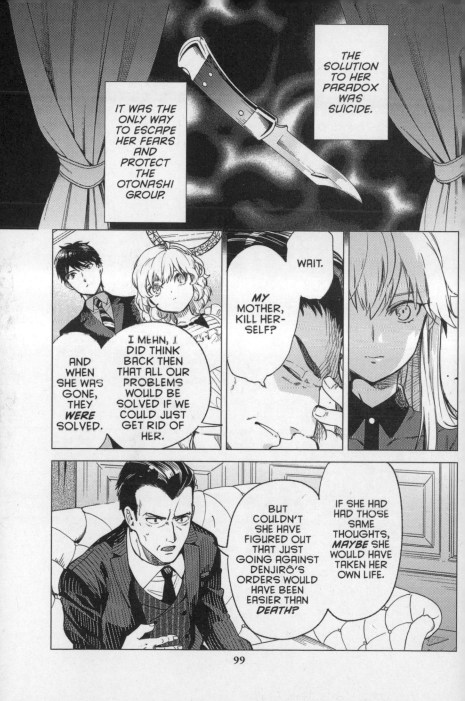

WHEN SOMEONE IS UNDER ENOUGH PRESSURE, THEY OFTEN RUSH TO THE NEAREST ESCAPE ROUTE.
HUMAN RELATIONS
WORK
STRESS
PRESSURE
PEOPLE OFTEN SAY AFTER THE FACT THAT THEY SHOULD HAVE JUST QUIT THEIR JOB.
THEY SHOULD HAVE JUST CUT THE TOXIC PEOPLE OUT OF THEIR LIVES.
IT'S EASY TO TALK.
BUT FOR THE PERSON WHO'S GOING THROUGH IT, THE SENSE OF RESPONSIBILITY AND FEAR OF REPERCUSSIONS MAKES IT IMPOSSIBLE TO TAKE SUCH ACTION.
THAT'S WHAT MAKES SUICIDE SO APPEALING—IT FREES THEM FROM RESPONSIBILITY, AND THEY'LL NEVER KNOW THE REPERCUSSIONS.

IF THEY HAVE SOMEONE TO SHARE THE BURDEN OF RESPONSIBILITY, OR TO TALK TO ABOUT POSSIBLE CONSEQUENCES, THAT WOULD CHANGE THINGS.
BUT PERHAPS SUMI-SAN DIDN'T HAVE SUCH A CONFI-DANT?
...
DYING WHEN SHE DID WAS CONVE-NIENT FOR EVERYONE, INCLUDING GRAND-MOTHER.
DAD SAID SO, TOO.
SHE DIED AT A GOOD TIME. SHE WAS LUCKY.
AND IN THAT CASE, I WOULD BELIEVE THAT DEATH APPEALED TO HER.

BUT GRAND-MOTHER COULDN'T JUST KILL HERSELF. IT WASN'T THAT SIMPLE.
IF THE PRESIDENT OF A BIG CORPO-RATION COMMITTED SUICIDE, IT WOULD BE A HUGE SCANDAL.
AND IT WOULD REFLECT POORLY ON THE COMPANY, TOO.
THERE'S NO WAY SHE COULD LET THAT HAPPEN— SHE WANTED TO **PROTECT** THE GROUP.
SO SHE NEEDED TO DIE IN A WAY THAT WASN'T OBVIOUSLY INTEN-TIONAL.
SO YOU'RE SAYING SHE KILLED HERSELF AND MADE IT LOOK LIKE HOMICIDE,
BY DIS-GUISING IT AS A MUG-GING?
THANK YOU VERY MUCH.

SHE WAS ALONE WHEN SHE LEFT THE MASSAGE CLINIC.
GRANDMOTHER CHOSE A TIME WHEN NO ONE WOULD BE AROUND, AND NO ONE WOULD COME WALKING BY.
AND NO ONE WOULD BE OUT TO SEE HER ON THOSE RESIDENTIAL STREETS.
AND SHE PUT HER PLAN INTO ACTION.
TOSS
TUMBLE
TUMBLE
TUMBLE

SHE HAD TAKEN ALL OF THE MONEY OUT OF HER WALLET AHEAD OF TIME. SHE THREW THE WALLET AND OPEN PURSE ON THE GROUND...
...TO MAKE IT LOOK LIKE A MUGGER HAD TAKEN THE BAG, REMOVED THE MONEY FROM THE WALLET, AND FLED.
THEN SHE TOOK HOLD OF THE KNIFE SHE HAD SECRETLY BROUGHT WITH HER.
BUT I THOUGHT THERE WERE NO FINGER-PRINTS ON THE KNIFE HANDLE?
IF YOU WRAP THE KNIFE IN THE HEM OF YOUR JACKET, YOU CAN GRAB THE HANDLE WITH-OUT LEAVING FINGER-PRINTS.
THEN, TO REALLY CONVINCE PEOPLE THAT IT WAS A HOMICIDE, SHE SHOUTED HER FINAL WORDS.

WHAM
!
THIEF!
SOMEBODY, HELP!
THAT MAN! THE MAN IN THE BLACK COAT! ARREST HIM!
ZH ZH
HE WENT TOWARD THE STATION!
NOW NO ONE WOULD EVER SUSPECT IT WAS SUICIDE.
GRANDMOTHER'S PLAN WAS ALMOST COMPLETE.
BUT IF SHE MADE IT LOOK LIKE A MURDER, THE POLICE WOULD HAVE TO INVESTIGATE.

ZH

THUD

IF ANYONE FROM THE OTONASHI GROUP BECAME A PRIME SUSPECT, THE COMPANY IMAGE WOULD STILL BE DAMAGED.

BECAUSE OF THAT, SHE MADE SURE IT HAPPENED...
...WHEN ALL OF THE LIKELY SUSPECTS HAD AN ALIBI.

THE PIECES DO ALL FIT.
BUT IF MOM KILLED HERSELF,
WHY WOULD DAD SAY THAT ***HE'S*** THE KILLER?

I THINK GRANDFATHER MIGHT HAVE INTENTIONALLY LED HER ON.
HE MADE GRANDMOTHER WANT TO KILL HERSELF.
HE DELIBERATELY POINTED THINGS OUT TO HER THAT WOULD MAKE HER THINK SUICIDE WAS THE BEST OPTION.
AND MAYBE HE'S CONVINCED THAT HE WAS THE ONE WHO GAVE HER THAT FINAL PUSH—
THE LAST PIECE OF INFORMATION THAT SENT HER OVER THE EDGE.
OF COURSE.

IF SHE KNEW THAT EVERY ONE OF HER CHILDREN WAS PLOTTING TO KILL HER...
THAT WOULD BE THE LAST STRAW.
SHE ALREADY SENSED THAT SHE WAS RUNNING THE BUSINESS INTO THE GROUND.
IF SHE REALIZED THAT THE THINGS SHE WAS DOING TO MAKE HER CHILDREN HAPPY WERE COMPLETELY BACKFIRING...
SHE MIGHT HAVE DECIDED TO KILL HERSELF ON THE SPOT.

IN ANY CASE, HER CHILDREN *DID* ALL WANT HER DEAD.
IF GRAND-FATHER DELIB-ERATELY POINTED THAT OUT TO HER,

THEN IT WOULD BE FAIR TO SAY THAT HE IS THE ONE WHO KILLED HER.

SLUMP
IN OTHER WORDS, MY BROTHER AND I, AND KAORUKO-NÊSAN AND KÔYA-SAN...
...ALL HELPED TO KILL MOM. IS THAT WHAT THIS ALL MEANS?

NO, NOT NECES-SARILY.

HE MAY BE POWERFUL, BUT WE DON'T KNOW THAT THE CHAIRMAN KNEW.
I ASSUME YOU WERE ALL PLAN-NING YOUR MURDERS VERY CARE-FULLY, BEHIND CLOSED DOORS.

HE MAY HAVE SIMPLY CREATED FALSE EVIDENCE ...
...TO CONVINCE SUMI-SAN THAT HER CHILDREN WERE PLOTTING TO KILL HER, IN ORDER TO DRIVE HER TO SUICIDE.
IT MAKES MORE SENSE TO THINK HIS LIE JUST HAPPENED TO COINCIDE WITH THE TRUTH.

THAT'S AWFULLY CHARI-TABLE OF YOU.

BUT WE DO HOLD SOME OF THE RESPONSIBILITY. WE CAN'T PUT IT ALL ON DAD.

WE DON'T HAVE ANY PROOF THAT THIS IS TRUE.
I'M SURE GRAND-MOTHER WOULD HAVE BEEN EXTREMELY CAREFUL NOT TO LEAVE ANY EVIDENCE.

IWANAGA-SAN WAS RIGHT.
WE PROBABLY WOULDN'T HAVE ACCEPTED THIS STORY IF GRANDFATHER HAD JUST COME OUT AND TOLD US.
IF WE DIDN'T THINK OF GRANDFATHER AS THE KILLER,
IF WE DIDN'T LEARN THAT EVERYONE HAD A PLOT TO KILL GRANDMOTHER,
IF WE DIDN'T LOOK OBJECTIVELY AT THE TOUGH SPOT GRANDMOTHER WAS IN,
WE WOULD NEVER HAVE BELIEVED ANY OF THIS.
AM I RIGHT IN ASSUMING THAT GRANDFATHER ASKED YOU TO LEAD US TO THE RIGHT ANSWER?
CHAIRMAN OTONASHI DIDN'T SEE A NEED FOR THAT.

DO THE TWO OF YOU AGREE WITH RION-SAN'S EXPLANA- TION?
IF SO, I WILL DECLARE THIS THE FINAL ANSWER AND PRESENT IT TO CHAIRMAN OTONASHI AT NOON TOMORROW.

I DOUBT WE'LL COME UP WITH A BETTER ONE.
AGREED.

THEN WHAT SHALL WE DO ABOUT DIVIDING THE INHERI- TANCE?
IT WAS RION-SAN WHO CONSTRUCTED THIS EXPLANATION, BUT SHALL I PROCEED WITH THE RANKINGS YOU PREVIOUSLY AGREED UPON?

I TRIED TO KILL MY OWN MOTHER—WHAT RIGHT DO I HAVE TO DEMAND PRIORITY IN THE INHERITANCE?

I'M SURE KAORUKO WOULD FEEL THE SAME WAY.
IF SHE HAD THE GALL TO DEMAND PRIORITY AFTER THIS, SHE WOULDN'T HAVE BEEN AFRAID TO COME HERE IN THE FIRST PLACE.

WHO EVEN NEEDS TOP PRIORITY ANYMORE?

GRAND-FATHER CAN DIVIDE THE INHERITANCE IN WHAT-EVER WAY HE THINKS IS BEST.
SKFF
SKFF
THEN I WILL ASK THE CHAIR-MAN TO DO JUST THAT.

RION-SAN.
WILL YOU BE PRESENTING THIS EXPLANA-TION TO THE CHAIRMAN YOURSELF?

I WOULDN'T MIND TELLING HIM FOR YOU.

HMPH

I'LL TELL HIM MYSELF.

IF *YOU* TELL HIM, YOU'LL JUST MAKE IT SOUND MORE SPITEFUL AND MEAN.

THE NAME RION HAS SUCH A NICE RING TO IT.

IT'S LIKE A COMBINATION OF *RISU** AND LION—CUTE AND COURAGEOUS, JUST LIKE YOU.

WHY DO YOU HAVE TO INTERPRET IT LIKE THAT?

IT'S JUST THE JAPANESE PRONUNCIATION OF THE ENGLISH SPELLING OF LION.

*JAPANESE FOR "SQUIRREL"

NII-SAN ALWAYS DID LIKE LIONS.
IF HE'D HAD A BOY, HE WOULD HAVE NAMED HIM LEO.
YOU REALLY DO KNOW RYÔMA-SAN.
Heh.
WHY DON'T YOU TAKE THIS OPPOR-TUNITY TO RECONCILE?
GULP
I'LL THINK ABOUT IT.
BUT FIRST, I'LL VISIT MOM'S GRAVE.
SHE WAS PROTECTING THE THINGS SHE NEEDED TO PROTECT IN THE BEST WAY SHE KNEW HOW.
NOW THAT I UNDERSTAND THAT, I NEED TO MOURN HER PROP-ERLY.

AND I SHOULDN'T WASTE ANY TIME IN TELLING KAORUKO.
BUT MAYBE I SHOULD WAIT UNTIL TOMORROW, AFTER THE CHAIRMAN CONFIRMS IT.

THE NEXT DAY
AND THAT'S OUR EXPLANA-TION.
HOW DID WE DO, GRAND-FATHER?

I SHOULD HAVE ARRANGED AN OPPORTUNITY LIKE THIS ONE SOONER.
RYÔMA, SUSUMU. KAORUKO, KÔYA-KUN.
I SEE NOW THAT FOR YEARS, I HAVE BURDENED YOU WITH AN EXCESS OF GUILT.
SIGH
ふぅ

YOUR ANSWER IS CORRECT.
BUT I DID NOT KNOW THAT YOU HAD ALL PLANNED TO KILL SUMI-SAN YOURSELVES.
THAT WAS PURE COINCI-DENCE.

STILL, I'M GLAD I EXECUTED MY PLAN TO DO AWAY WITH SUMI-SAN BEFORE ANY OF YOU COULD CARRY OUT YOUR OWN.
BECAUSE THIS WAY, I AT LEAST MANAGED TO STOP YOU FROM KILLING YOUR OWN MOTHER.

BUT THE FACT REMAINS THAT NII-SAN AND I, AND KAORUKO-NÊSAN AND KÔYA-SAN, ARE ALL GUILTY.
EVEN IF THERE IS NO PROOF, AND IT'S TOO LATE TO TRY US IN A COURT OF LAW.

AND DAD, I'M SURE MOM DOESN'T HOLD IT AGAINST YOU.
AT THE TIME,
IT WAS THE ONLY CHOICE ANY OF US HAD.

EVERYONE HAS EXPERIENCED THE DESIRE TO KILL SOMEONE.
SOMETIMES, WE EVEN REACH FOR A WEAPON.
BUT THERE'S A LINE, AND WHETHER YOU CROSS THAT LINE OR NOT MAKES ALL THE DIFFERENCE.
I ACCEPT THE BLAME FOR KILLING SUMI-SAN.
ALL I WANT FROM YOU IS TO STAND WITNESS TO MY PAINFUL DEATH.
I HAVEN'T TOLD ANY OF YOU THIS YET,
BUT I HAVE BEEN SUFFERING FROM SEVERAL MALIGNANT TUMORS FOR SOME TIME NOW.

TMP
THIS ILLNESS, AND THIS PAIN, ARE THE PRICE I PAY FOR KILLING SUMI-SAN.
IN A FEW MONTHS, I'LL HARDLY BE ABLE TO STAND.
I WILL SUFFER INTENSE PAIN, AND I WILL MEET A CRUEL END. THAT IS MY PROGNOSIS.

THEY TELL ME THEY WOULD LIKE TO RENOUNCE ANY RIGHTS TO PRIORITY IN THE INHERITANCE.

IT WAS RION-SAN WHO CONTRIBUTED THE MOST TO FINDING THE ANSWER.

AND SHE WOULD LIKE FOR YOU TO DISTRIBUTE THE INHERITANCE HOWEVER YOU SEE FIT.

HOW SELFLESS OF THEM.

NO, I BELIEVE THEY MADE THE RIGHT CHOICE.

I SUSPECT YOU WERE THE ONE WHO TRULY CONTRIB-UTED THE MOST.

KOTOKO-SAN, I'M GLAD I ASKED YOU.

YOU HAVE MY THANKS.

I BELIEVE YOUR THANKS MAY BE PREMATURE.

IF YOU HAD KILLED YOUR WIFE BY YOUR OWN HAND,
I WOULD NOT HAVE HAD TO INTERJECT MY OWN UNSOLICITED OPINION.
BUT YOU USED A VERY UNIQUE METHOD.
THAT WAS NOT RIGHT.
AND IT IS IMPORTANT THAT YOU UNDERSTAND THAT.
AT THIS MOMENT, YOU BELIEVE YOU DID A GOOD THING IN CHOOSING THAT METHOD.
BECAUSE, AS YOU SAID MERE MOMENTS AGO, YOU PREVENTED YOUR CHILDREN FROM KILLING THEIR OWN MOTHER.

AND IF THAT IS HOW YOU FEEL, THEN YOU HAVE NOT TRULY REPENTED ...
...OF YOUR PAST SUCCESS, OR OF THE CHOICE THAT LED TO IT.
RION-SAN.
YOU DETERMINED THAT SUMI OTONASHI-SAN KILLED HERSELF.
THEN WHY DID SHE NOT CHOOSE TO MAKE IT LOOK LIKE AN ACCIDENT?
...BE-CAUSE ...
...
SHE CARELESSLY RAN OUT INTO TRAFFIC TO PICK UP SOME-THING SHE DROPPED.
HER FOOT SLIPPED AND SHE FELL FROM A TRAIN PLATFORM ONTO THE TRACKS.
IT'S EASY TO DRESS A SUICIDE UP LIKE AN ACCIDENT IF THE VICTIM SO DESIRES.

IF SOME-
ONE WHO
OUTWARDLY
SHOWS NO
SIGNS OF
SUICIDAL
TENDENCIES
DIED IN SUCH
A WAY,
IT WOULD
LIKELY BE
RULED AN
ACCIDENT,
EVEN IF IT WAS
SOMEWHAT
UNNATURAL.
CLACK
K—
KOTOKO-
SAN.

THEN THE
POLICE
WOULDN'T
BOTHER
WITH A
THOROUGH
INVESTI-
GATION.
AND SHE
WOULDN'T
HAVE TO
WORRY
ABOUT
ALIBIS FOR
ANYONE.
...
CLACK
CLACK
AND IN FACT,
KAORUKO-
SAN ALMOST
DIDN'T HAVE
AN ALIBI.
IF SHE
HADN'T
ACTUALLY
BROKEN HER
LEG, SHE
WOULD STILL
HAVE BEEN A
SUSPECT.

FURTHER-
MORE, IF THE
POLICE PER-
FORMED THE
INVESTIGATION
PROPERLY,
THEY MAY HAVE
DISCOVERED A
COVER-UP.
IT WOULD
HAVE BEEN
VERY RISKY
TO MAKE
HER DEATH
LOOK LIKE A
HOMICIDE.

WHICH IS TO SAY, SHE MADE NO SUCH EFFORTS.

SUMI OTONASHI-SAN DID NOT KILL HERSELF

IT WAS, IN FACT, A MURDER.

NOW THEN, ALLOW ME TO IMPLICATE THE REAL KILLER.

Hmm.
What should we have for dinner?
I suggest body sushi.
Male or female.
~Meal Planning~

CHAPTER 28: "SLEEPING MURDER PART FOUR"

THE REAL KILLER...?

Whew.
WE FINALLY MADE IT TO THIS POINT.

THREE WEEKS PRIOR

YOU PROMISED GÔICHI THAT WHEN YOU KILLED HER, YOU WOULD "MAKE SURE NO ONE SUSPECTS YOU OR YOUR FAMILY."
BUT IT ISN'T EASY TO CLEAR SUCH PEOPLE OF SUSPICION WHEN YOU KILL A PERSON.
ASSUMING YOU WANTED TO ESTABLISH ALIBIS FOR ALL OF THEM, YOU WOULD HAVE HAD TO ACQUAINT YOURSELF WITH ALL OF THEIR PLANS AND SCHEDULES.
WHICH MAKES A FABRICATED ACCIDENT OR ILLNESS THE EASIEST AND SAFEST WAY TO DO THE DEED.
YOU DIDN'T KILL SUMI OTONASHI-SAN.
YOU ONLY PRETENDED YOU DID, AND REPORTED BACK TO GÔICHI TO MAKE HIM KEEP HIS END OF THE BARGAIN.

MURMUR
ザワ
HOW PERCEP-TIVE OF YOU,
MY LADY.
SNAP
ゴキ
SNA-SNAP
ゴキキ
ZH
ZH
ズズ
POOF
ドロン
I DID NOT KILL THAT WOMAN.
BUT I HADN'T PLANNED ON TRICKING GÔICHI AT FIRST.

THAT EVENING, I'D SET OUT TO KILL THAT SUMI WOMAN, AND WAS THUS DISGUISED AS A STRAY DOG.
I'D BEEN TAILING THE WOMAN SINCE THE DAY I MADE THE DEAL.
BUT THAT WAS THE FIRST TIME SHE WAS ALONE.
IF I LET THIS CHANCE GET AWAY, THERE'S NO TELLING WHEN I'LL GET ANOTHER ONE.
CLACK
CLACK
STARE
I HAVE TO FINISH HER ONCE AND FOR ALL.
MY PLAN WAS TO TRANSFORM INTO A STRAY DOG AND ATTACK THE WOMAN. SHE'D RUN AND I'D GO AFTER HER.
THEN, WHEN I'D ATTRACTED A FEW WITNESSES, I'D BITE HER IN THE THROAT.
OR I'D CHASE HER OUT INTO THE STREET AND GET HER HIT BY A CAR.
I ALSO FIGURED I COULD WAIT UNTIL SHE WAS STANDING BY THE ROAD, BUMP INTO HER FROM BEHIND—STILL AS A DOG—AND KNOCK HER INTO THE STREET.

MM-HM.
MM-HM.
MM-HM.
YES, THAT WOULD DEFINITELY FULFILL YOUR END OF THE DEAL.
BUT THEN SOMETHING HAPPENED.
BEFORE MY VERY EYES...
...THE WOMAN WAS STABBED TO DEATH—SHE WAS AMBUSHED BY ANOTHER HUMAN.

BAM
THE KILLER MADE SURE SHE WAS DEAD, THEN TOSSED ALL HER STUFF ON THE GROUND,
TOOK HER MONEY,
AND RAN AWAY, JUST LIKE THAT.
TEP TEP
AAHH!
ZSH
WHAT HAVE YOU DONE?!
NOW MY DEAL WITH THE HUMAN WILL BE RUINED!
GRIT
I HAVE TO DO SOME-THING!

SNAP
SNAP
KRAK
CRR
THIEF!

SOMEBODY, HELP!
THAT MAN!
THAT MAN IN THE BLACK COAT! ARREST HIM!
HE WENT TOWARD THE STATION!
POOF
KA-CHAK
FSH
THMP
THMP
LOOK, A WOMAN ON THE GROUND!
SOMEBODY CALL AN AMBULANCE!

SO THE SHOUTS DIDN'T COME FROM THE VICTIM—IT WAS YOU ALL ALONG.
FLUTTER ぱた
FLUTTER ぱた
FAN: GOAT
YES.
THE WOMAN WAS PRACTICALLY DEAD AFTER THE FIRST STAB TO THE CHEST.
TO THINK, A FOX SPIRIT FALSIFYING EVIDENCE ON THE SCENE.
AND YEARS LATER, I HAVE TO MAKE IT ALL MAKE SENSE... THIS WILL NOT BE EASY.
THERE WERE NO CLUES OR EVIDENCE ON THE SCENE.
AND THE KILLER WOULD NEVER COME FOR-WARD.
I MAY NOT HAVE KILLED HER MYSELF, BUT MY TARGET WAS STILL DEAD.
HMM...
I FIGURED NOBODY WOULD MIND IF I TOLD HIM I'D DONE IT.
SO I WENT TO HIM AND ASKED HIM TO KEEP HIS END OF THE BARGAIN.

SINCE I DID DO EVERYTHING IN MY POWER TO MAKE SURE NO ONE SUS-PECTED HIM OR HIS FAMILY, IT WASN'T AN ENTIRELY UNFAIR REQUEST.
SO, YOU SAW THE KILLER'S FACE.
AND YOU KNEW WHO IT WAS.
AND THAT'S WHY YOU HAD TO PRETEND TO BE THE VICTIM, AND MAKE SURE PEOPLE HEARD YOU SCREAM—TO PROTECT THE MURDERER.
I SEE. IN THAT CASE...
YES.
I'D DONE MY HOMEWORK. I RECOGNIZED THE KILLER.
TWITCH
SNAP
SO I SHOUTED, AND MADE SURE EVERY-ONE THOUGHT IT WAS A MAN.
WHICH MEANS THE REAL KILLER...
THEN WHO KILLED SUMI-SAN?

THE MAN'S DAUGHTER.
A WOMAN NAMED KAORUKO.

THE REAL KILLER WAS KAORUKO-SAN.
IT WAS ASSUMED THAT KAORUKO-SAN COULD NOT POS-SIBLY HAVE COMMITTED THE CRIME, BUT AS WE DISCUSSED YESTERDAY,
IF SHE FALSIFIED THE TIME OF HER FRACTURE, THE IMPOSSIBLE BECOMES POSSIBLE.
IN REALITY, SHE DID DO JUST THAT, AND SHE MURDERED SUMI-SAN.

I NEED TO TALK TO YOU ABOUT MY RELATIONSHIP WITH KÔYA-SAN.

CLACK

I HAD TO COME OUT LIKE THIS, OR I'D NEVER GET A MOMENT ALONE WITH YOU.

CLACK

KAORUKO-SAN MOST LIKELY WAITED TO AMBUSH SUMI-SAN ON THE ROAD BETWEEN THE MASSAGE CLINIC AND THE STATION.

THEN SHE MARCHED RIGHT UP TO HER.

CLACK

AS FOR SUMI-SAN, THIS WAS HER DAUGHTER, AND SHE WOULD HAVE REALIZED THAT THIS WAS THE ONLY WAY KAORUKO-SAN COULD DISCUSS PRIVATE MATTERS WITH HER.

SHE WOULD HAVE REMAINED UNGUARDED AS THE YOUNG WOMAN APPROACHED.

KAORUKO-SAN TOOK ADVANTAGE.
WHAM
HZ
WHAM

TO MAKE IT LOOK LIKE A MUGGING, SHE PULLED THE WALLET OUT OF HER MOTHER'S PURSE,
ZH ズ…
REMOVED ALL THE MONEY FROM IT, AND RAN FROM THE SCENE.
ZHRR ずる
IT WOULDN'T HAVE TAKEN 30 SECONDS.

B-DMP
...! AUNT KAORUKO...
KILLED GRANDMOTHER...?
KÔYA-SAN.
I ASSUME YOU ARE AWARE OF KAORUKO-SAN'S CRIME?
WHEN I CALLED YOU ON THE BROKEN LEG PLOY, YOU DIDN'T TRY TO DENY IT.
INSTEAD, YOU ADMITTED THAT YOU *HAD* PLANNED THE MURDER, BUT CLAIMED THAT YOU'D FAILED. QUITE BRILLIANT, REALLY.

BUT ALL YOU OR KAORUKO-SAN COULD SEE IN IT WAS AN ATTEMPT TO RENDER HIS OWN JUDGMENT ON YOU, 23 YEARS AFTER THE FACT.

I'M SURE FOR THE TWO OF YOU, THIS CURRENT PLOT OF CHAIRMAN OTONASHI'S WAS NOTHING BUT A SOURCE OF CONSTANT DREAD.
THE CHAIRMAN'S ONLY INTENTION WAS TO CONVINCE YOU ALL OF HIS OWN CRIMES.

EVERY SINGLE WORD OUT OF HIS MOUTH...
...WOULD SOUND LIKE CONDEMNATION.

NEVER-THELESS,
THE POSSIBILITY REMAINED THAT THE CHAIRMAN HAD AN ENTIRELY DIFFERENT AIM IN MIND WHEN HE SET THIS ASSIGN-MENT.
THAT'S WHY YOU WATCHED SO CAREFULLY TO SEE HOW THE SITUATION WOULD UNFOLD.

EVENTUALLY, RYÔMA-SAN AND SUSUMU-SAN'S MURDER PLOT WAS EXPOSED.
THAT WAS AN UNEX-PECTED TWIST.

THEN, WHEN YOU REALIZED THAT I SUSPECTED THE TWO OF YOU AS WELL,
YOU MADE IT A POINT TO CONFESS.

THAT WAY, EVEN IF THE CHAIRMAN DID HAVE PROOF THAT YOU WERE PLANNING MURDER,
YOU COULD ESCAPE BLAME BY SAYING YOUR ATTEMPT FAILED.
THAT ALSO SERVED AS A WAY TO GAUGE HOW MUCH CHAIRMAN OTONASHI KNEW OF THE TRUTH.
FINALLY, RION-SAN PRESENTED HER THEORY AS TO HOW THE CHAIR-MAN COULD BE THE KILLER.
THIS IS WHERE YOU, KÔYA-SAN, STARTED TO THINK THAT PERHAPS THIS THEORETICAL PLAN HAD ACTUALLY BEEN PUT INTO ACTION,
BUT YOU TWO HAD KILLED SUMI-SAN BEFORE IT COULD REACH FRUITION.
JUST AS RYÔMA-SAN AND SUSUMU-SAN WERE UNABLE TO CARRY OUT THEIR OWN MURDER.

YOU DETERMINED THAT THIS BIZARRE SITUATION WAS THE RESULT OF THREE MURDER PLOTS COINCIDENTALLY MOVING FORWARD SIMULTANEOUSLY,
THAT CHAIRMAN OTONASHI JUST ASSUMED HIS OWN PLAN WAS THE ONE THAT HAD BEEN SUCCESSFUL,
AND THAT, THEREFORE, HE REALLY DID ONLY GIVE THIS ASSIGNMENT TO ATONE FOR HIS OWN CRIME.
I IMAGINE YOU FELT SOME SLIGHT RELIEF LAST NIGHT.
AND YOU CALLED KAORUKO-SAN TO GIVE HER THE NEWS.

THEN TODAY, CHAIRMAN OTONASHI ADMITTED TO HIS OWN PLOT.
AND YOU WERE READY TO LET HIM TAKE ALL THE BLAME...
...AS I'M SURE YOU TOLD KAORUKO-SAN YOU WOULD.
IF YOU HAD INTERRUPTED CHAIRMAN OTONASHI AND CONFESSED KAORUKO-SAN'S CRIME,
THERE WOULD HAVE BEEN NO NEED FOR *ME* TO TELL EVERYONE.
BUT CHAIRMAN OTONASHI DID SAY,
"MURDER BEING ONCE DONE, REQUIRES A SUITABLE PRICE BE PAID. EVEN IF THAT MURDER SOLVES ALL OF YOUR PROBLEMS, YOU WILL PAY A PRICE IN THE END."

SCRUNCH
IF, AFTER HEARING THAT,
YOU STILL INSIST ON MAINTAINING YOUR SILENCE,
THEN I MUST IMPART THE TRUTH.
IF FOR NOTHING ELSE...
...THAN TO SUPPORT CHAIRMAN OTONASHI'S CONVICTIONS.

IWANAGA-SAN.
WHAT IS THIS FARCE?
AREN'T YOU THE ONE WHO DENIED KAORUKO'S CULPABILITY JUST LAST NIGHT?
SUMI-SAN'S LAST WORDS STATED THAT THE MURDERER WAS A MAN.
WE EVEN PROVED THAT THE KILLER COULDN'T HAVE FAKED THE SHOUTS TO THROW PEOPLE OFF HIS TRAIL.
KAORUKO IS THE *LAST* PERSON WHO COULD HAVE COMMITTED THIS CRIME.
I'M SURE YOU AND YOUR WIFE...
...WERE VERY SURPRISED TO LEARN, LATER THAT NIGHT, THAT THE VICTIM'S SHOUTS WERE HEARD ON THE SCENE.
AND THAT THOSE SHOUTS WORKED TO YOUR ADVAN-TAGE.

PERHAPS YOU WENT SO FAR AS TO SUSPECT CHAIRMAN OTONASHI OF PULLING STRINGS,
TO MAKE SURE THE POLICE WERE GIVEN FALSE INFORMATION.
THIS WOULD HAVE MADE YOU ALL THE MORE AFRAID...
...THAT THIS MEETING WAS ABOUT HIS KNOWLEDGE OF YOUR CRIME.
BUT I ASSURE YOU, THOSE WORDS DID COME FROM SUMI-SAN.
SHE WANTED TO PROTECT HER DAUGHTER,
SO SHE USED THE LAST OF HER STRENGTH TO RAISE HER CRIES AND CONVINCE THE WORLD THAT SHE WAS KILLED BY A MALE MUGGER.

SHE TRIED TO SHIELD THE MURDERER FROM THE POLICE INVESTIGATION, BECAUSE IT WAS HER OWN DAUGHTER.
YOU DENIED THAT YESTER-DAY, TOO!
CLATTER
IF THE CRIME WAS PREMEDITATED, THE KILLER WOULD HAVE COVERED THE VICTIM'S MOUTH TO AVOID ATTRACTING ATTENTION.
AND HE WOULDN'T LEAVE THE SCENE UNTIL HE WAS SURE THE VICTIM WAS DEAD—THAT WAY HE WOULDN'T LEAVE ANY CLUES!
KÔYA-SAN!
SKFF
SKFF
IF IT WAS PREMEDI-TATED, AND THE KILLER KNEW THE VICTIM, THE VICTIM WOULD HAVE HAD NO CHANCE TO SCREAM!
THAT'S HOW WE DETERMINED THAT IT HAD TO BE AN UNINTENTIONAL SLAYING BY SOMEONE WHO HAD NEVER SEEN THE VICTIM BEFORE!

IT WAS HER FIRST MURDER.
KAORUKO-SAN DIDN'T KNOW HOW TO REALLY CONFIRM THAT SUMI-SAN HAD DIED.
WHEN SHE SAW THAT HER VICTIM HAD FALLEN AND STOPPED MOVING, SHE ASSUMED ALL WAS WELL.
FUBUKI DID HONOR HIS AGREEMENT WITH THE CHAIRMAN.
IT WAS HIS IMPERSONATED CRIES THAT PROTECTED KAORUKO.
BUT SUMI-SAN HADN'T QUITE BREATHED HER LAST—SHE SQUEEZED OUT THE LAST OF HER DYING ENERGY...
A MOTHER'S LOVE FOR HER DAUGHTER IS A POWERFUL THING.
STOP MAKING THINGS UP!

B-DMP
DID KAORUKO-SAN TAKE THE VICTIM'S PULSE?
HUFF
HUFF
DID SHE CHECK HER BREATHING?
I ASSUME SHE WORE GLOVES, SO AS NOT TO LEAVE PRINTS ON THE KNIFE.
HUFF
HUFF
SHE WAS PLANNING THIS ALL ALONG.
THAT'S WHY SHE LED ME TO THAT FAKE EXPLANATION.
ALL SO SHE COULD...
DID SHE USE THOSE GLOVED HANDS TO MAKE ABSOLUTELY SURE?

...DRIVE UNCLE KÔYA INTO A CORNER.
KAORUKO TOLD ME SHE CHECKED HER BREATHING!
THERE ARE ALSO WITNESS TESTIMONIES STATING THAT THE BODY WAS STILL WARM WHEN THE RESIDENTS RAN UP.
IF IT WAS ONLY A FEW MINUTES AFTER, SHE'D STILL HAVE SOME BODY HEAT!

BODIES DON'T GO COLD THAT QUICKLY!
BUT MANY PEOPLE HEARD THE VICTIM SCREAM.
SUMI-SAN WAS STILL ALIVE.
OF COURSE, WE'LL NEVER KNOW IF IT WAS THE LOVE OF A PARENT,
OR CONCERN FOR THE OTONASHI GROUP'S CORPORATE IMAGE,
THAT LED HER TO HIDE HER DAUGHTER'S CRIME WITH THOSE SHOUTS.
SHIVER
SHIVER
SHIVER
SHIVER

NOW THEN.
AFTER ALL OF MY INSINUATIONS AND IMPLICATIONS YESTERDAY, AS WELL AS THE BARRAGE OF UNEXPECTED TWISTS,
EVEN YOU, KÔYA-SAN, MUST BE MENTALLY EXHAUSTED.
AND THAT CAN LEAD TO MISTAKES.
THE MURDER HAPPENED 23 YEARS AGO. THERE IS NO EVIDENCE.
UNLESS WE CONVINCE THE KILLER TO VOICE SOMETHING ONLY HE COULD KNOW, ALL WE CAN DO IS TALK IN CIRCLES.
YOU SAID SOMETHING A MOMENT AGO, KÔYA-SAN.
"KAORUKO TOLD ME SHE CHECKED HER BREATHING!"

CHAIRMAN OTONASHI.
AS YOU CAN SEE, KAORUKO-SAN IS THE MURDERER.
AND KŌYA-SAN IS HER ACCOMPLICE.

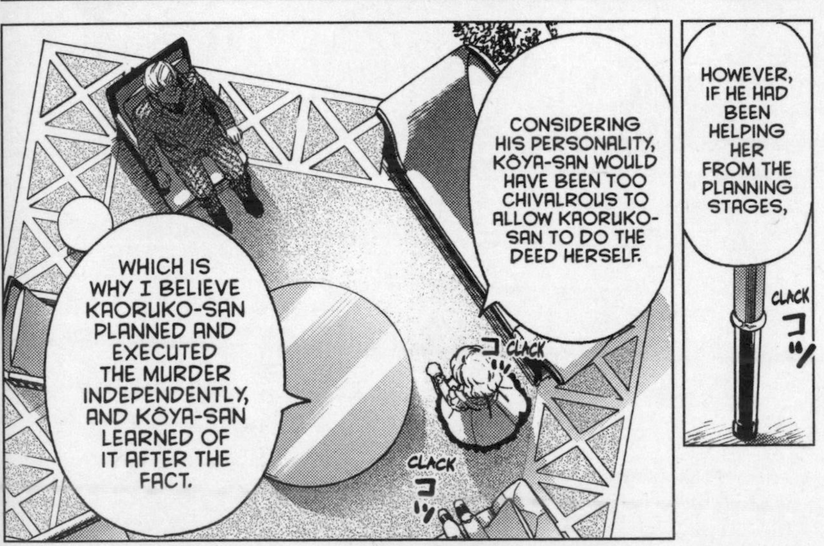
HOWEVER, IF HE HAD BEEN HELPING HER FROM THE PLANNING STAGES,
コッ
CLACK
CONSIDERING HIS PERSONALITY, KÔYA-SAN WOULD HAVE BEEN TOO CHIVALROUS TO ALLOW KAORUKO-SAN TO DO THE DEED HERSELF.
コ
CLACK
WHICH IS WHY I BELIEVE KAORUKO-SAN PLANNED AND EXECUTED THE MURDER INDEPENDENTLY, AND KÔYA-SAN LEARNED OF IT AFTER THE FACT.
コッ
CLACK

WHEN YOU GAVE THIS ASSIGNMENT, SHE WAS TERRIFIED.
AND PERHAPS THAT FEAR PROMPTED HER TO TELL KÔYA-SAN FOR THE FIRST TIME, 23 YEARS LATER.
コッ
CLACK
THAT WOULD MAKE HIM EVEN MORE DESPERATE TO COVER FOR HER.

THE CASE HAS PASSED ITS STATUTE OF LIMITATIONS, SO WHATEVER HAPPENS NOW IS A MATTER OF THE FAMILY'S AND YOUR OWN CONVICTIONS.
DO WITH THESE FACTS WHAT YOU WILL.
...TO SHOW YOU THAT YOU HAD TRUSTED IN POWERS YOU SHOULD NEVER HAVE RELIED ON.
AS I STATED IN THE BEGIN-NING, WHEN WE LEAVE THIS HOTEL, WE WILL FORGET THE ENTIRE AFFAIR.
I ONLY WANTED...

WHAT YOU DID DEFIES ORDER,
THUS CREATING A KARMIC NEED FOR YOU TO FACE THIS TRUTH.
IF YOU HAD ATTEMPTED TO KILL YOUR WIFE WITH YOUR OWN HANDS,

OR IF YOU HAD RESISTED THE EXTRA-LOGICAL TEMPTATION,
EVEN THOUGH YOUR DAUGHTER WAS THE KILLER,

YOU COULD HAVE LIVED OUT YOUR LIFE BELIEVING THAT YOUR WIFE WAS KILLED BY A RANDOM MUGGER.

KURÔ-SENPAI.
IT IS TIME THAT WE OUTSIDERS TAKE OUR LEAVE.
BOW
CLACK
CLACK
WAIT.

DO YOU THINK I'M JUST GOING TO LET YOU GO?

!!
!
JOLT
KÔYA-SAN!
DON'T DO ANYTHING HASTY!
IT DOESN'T MATTER— IF THE POLICE FIND OUT, THEY CAN'T DO ANYTHING!
NONE OF US CAN BLAME YOU FOR WHAT YOU DID! AND I WOULD NEVER TELL ANYONE!

YES.
I TRUST YOU, THE CHAIRMAN, AND RION-SAN.
BECAUSE *YOU* BELONG TO THE OTONASHI FAMILY.
BUT...
...*THEY* DON'T.
FIRST OF ALL,
KRK
THERE WAS NO REASON FOR THEM TO REVEAL THE TRUTH.
BUT SHE DELIBERATELY DID IT ANYWAY. SHE MUST BE AFTER SOME-THING.

NO...
IT NEVER MADE ANY SENSE FOR THEM TO BE HERE!
YES, THE STATUTE OF LIMITATIONS HAS EXPIRED, BUT IF PEOPLE FIND OUT, THERE WILL ABSOLUTELY BE SOCIAL CONSE-QUENCES!
GRRRG
THESE OUT-SIDERS ...
SHIVER
SHIVER
UN-CLE ...
SHIVER
DON'T ...
THIS KOTOKO IWANAGA— I CAN'T TRUST HER. I DON'T KNOW WHAT SHE'LL DO.
YOU ALL KNOW I CAN'T LET HER LEAVE HERE!

DO?! I WON'T DO ANYTHING.
I SEE HOW MUCH YOU LOVE AND CHERISH KAORUKO-SAN.
AND SHE WAS WILLING TO COMMIT MURDER TO HAVE A FUTURE WITH YOU.
HOW COULD I STAND IN THE WAY OF SUCH A BEAUTIFUL ROMANCE?
THE GODS OF LOVE WOULD SMITE ME.
I WOULD NOT WANT TO RUIN MY RELATIONSHIP WITH KURÔ-SENPAI FOR THAT.
WHICH IS WHY I HAVE NO INTENTION...
...OF HAVING ANY FURTHER INVOLVEMENT IN THIS CASE.
DON'T UPSET HIM WITH YOUR RIDICULOUSNESS.
BAP
PFFT!
GRR
RIDICULOUSNESS?! I WAS ONLY STATING THAT I HAVE PERSONAL REASONS FOR NOT GETTING INVOLVED!

UM.
すッ ZOOM
SHIELD
I KNOW HOW IWANAGA MAY SEEM TO YOU, BUT TRUST ME, SHE REALLY WON'T DO ANYTHING.
CLACK
CLACK
ギ GRG
DON'T MOVE.
THIS ISN'T AN EMPTY THREAT.
CLACK
CLACK
YOU'RE THE ONE UPSETTING HIM, SENPAI.
I ADMIRE YOUR COURAGE, BUT IS THAT GIRL REALLY WORTH RISKING YOUR LIFE FOR?
UNFORTUNATELY, *MY* LIFE WOULDN'T REALLY CONSTITUTE A RISK.

BANG

CRASH

CRUNCH
THERE'S NO TURNING BACK NOW.
CHAK
YOU AND YOUR BOYFRIEND WERE BOTH WRONG.

NO, I'M RIGHT.
AND YOU CAN STILL TURN BACK.

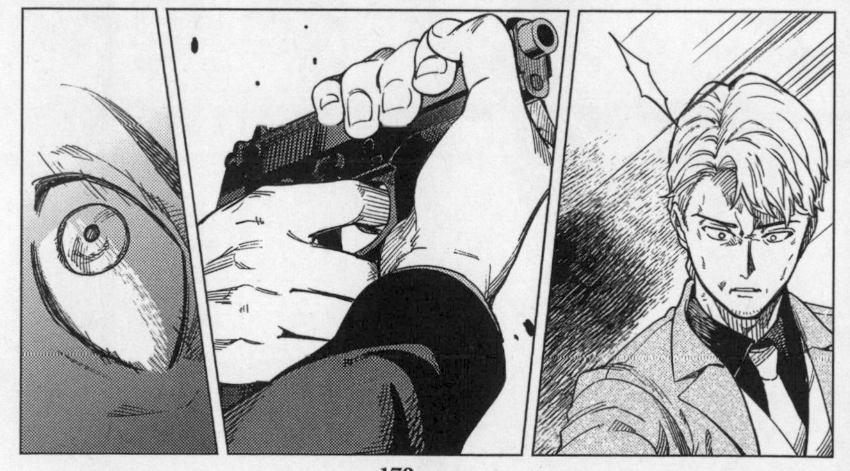

SNATCH

I TOLD YOU MY LIFE WOULDN'T CONSTITUTE A RISK.
HOW?
HOW ARE YOU ALIVE?
I SHOT YOU IN THE HEAD!
THE BULLET WENT STRAIGHT THROUGH YOU—IT'S RIGHT THERE IN THE WALL!
UM, WELL.
IT'S LIKE, YOU KNOW, THAT THING.
YOU SEE IT IN HISTORICAL DRAMAS ALL THE TIME, WHERE THEY HIT PEOPLE WITH THE NON-LETHAL SIDE.
AND WHAT EXACTLY IS THE NON-LETHAL SIDE OF A BULLET?!

ひょい
YOINK
THE THINGS THAT HAPPENED HERE ARE LIKE THE VISIONS OF A WAKING DREAM.
PLEASE, JUST THINK OF US AS DENIZENS OF THAT DREAM.
ゴト
CLUNK
AS SUCH, WE ARE NEITHER BOUND BY THE LAWS AND RULES OF THIS WORLD, NOR DO WE HAVE ANY INTEREST IN THEM.
NOW THEN, EVERYONE. THIS TIME, I *WILL* BE TAKING MY LEAVE.

I HAVE NO INTENTION OF MAKING AN ENEMY OF THE OTONASHI GROUP.
CHAIRMAN OTONASHI, I LEAVE THE REST TO YOU.

SHUT
パタ…
THUD
ドッ

ザァァァ
ZSHHH
SEPTEMBER 18.
TWO WEEKS HAVE PASSED SINCE THAT MEETING.
TV: WORLD'S MOST SHOCKING QUIZ
DING-ALING
チャラララ~
HEY, EVERYBODY! THE SHOW'S STARTING! IT'S TIME FOR THE WORLD'S MOST SHOCKING QUIZ!
TODAY'S SUBJECT IS LOCKED-ROOM MURDERS!
THE DAY AFTER WE ALL LEARNED THE TRUTH OF WHAT HAPPENED 23 YEARS AGO,
AUNT KAORUKO TRIED TO KILL HERSELF.

UNCLE KÔYA FOUND HER SOON AFTER, AND GOT HER HELP IN TIME TO SAVE HER LIFE.

BUT SHE'S BEEN IN THE HOSPITAL EVER SINCE.

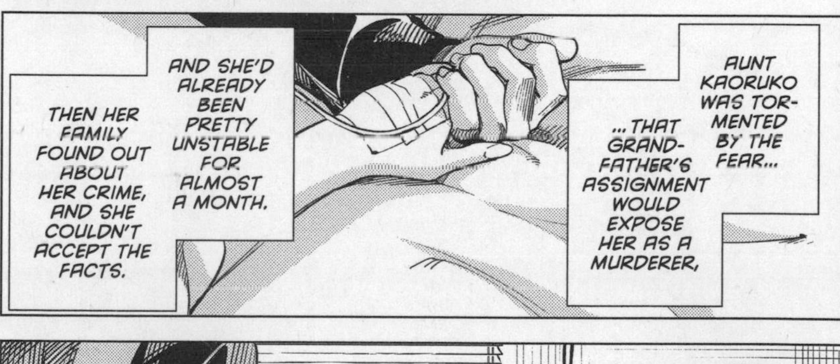

AUNT KAORUKO WAS TORMENTED BY THE FEAR...
...THAT GRANDFATHER'S ASSIGNMENT WOULD EXPOSE HER AS A MURDERER,
AND SHE'D ALREADY BEEN PRETTY UNSTABLE FOR ALMOST A MONTH.
THEN HER FAMILY FOUND OUT ABOUT HER CRIME, AND SHE COULDN'T ACCEPT THE FACTS.

AND I BET SHE'D FELT GUILTY FOR YEARS ABOUT KILLING HER MOTHER.

THE SHADOW WAS ALWAYS THERE.
23 YEARS AGO, THERE WAS A MURDER, AND THERE WAS A KILLER TO GO WITH IT.
THE FACTS WERE JUST SLEEPING, THAT'S ALL.
IF SHE HAD KEPT THE TRUTH TO HERSELF,
WE COULD HAVE AVOIDED THIS OUTCOME.
BUT SHE WOKE THE SLEEPING MURDER ANYWAY.
THERE'S SOMETHING ABOUT IT I CAN'T EXPLAIN.
IT'S LIKE KOTOKO IWANAGA HAS HER OWN SET OF CONVICTIONS AND RULES TO FOLLOW.
AND IF ANYONE GETS IN THE WAY, SHE SHOWS THEM NO MERCY.
SHE'S RUTHLESS...
SHUDDER
HINT
SO WHAT REALLY HAPPENED?!
I AM NEVER SOLVING MYSTERIES EVER AGAIN.
BEEP

ザア
ZSHHH
仕度中
SIGN: OPEN SOON
ガラ
UNCLE?
HI.
I HOPE YOU DON'T MIND I'M HERE.
STOPPED BY ON HIS WAY HOME FROM VISITING YOUR AUNT.
ぴょいこ
FWIP
WEL-COME.

I GUESS THE ONE GOOD THING TO COME OUT OF THIS IS THAT MY DAD AND UNCLE HAVE RECONCILED.
KÔYA-SAN IS SO DEVOTED, HE NEVER LEAVES KAORUKO-NÊSAN'S SIDE.

AND DAD... HE'S GETTING A LOT WORSE.
IT'S PROBABLY ALL THE EMOTIONAL STRAIN ON TOP OF THE CANCER.

I SEE...

GRANDFATHER PASSED OUT AFTER THE MEETING AND HAD TO GO TO THE HOSPITAL, TOO.

HE MEANT TO BE JUDGED FOR HIS CRIME, BUT INSTEAD HE EXPOSED AUNT KAORUKO'S.

HE WAS FORCED TO DECIDE IF HE WOULD HE RENDER JUDGMENT ACCORDING TO THE CONVICTIONS HE'D EXPRESSED WHEN THE MEETING STARTED.

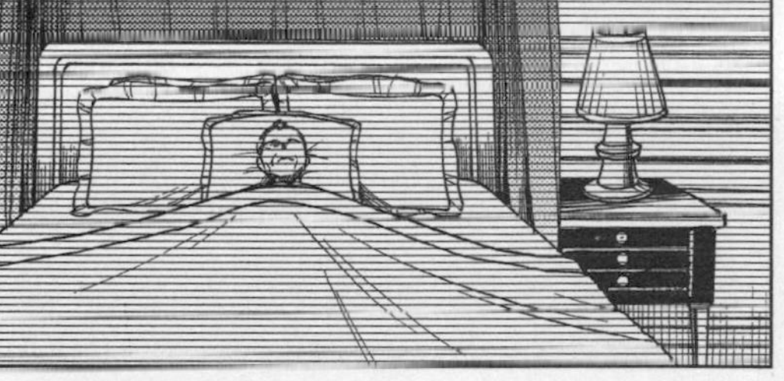

YOU COULD SAY IT WAS HIS OWN FAULT FOR BRINGING THAT HEIRESS INTO THIS.
AND NOW HIS GUILT OVER IT IS MAKING THE TIME HE HAS LEFT EVEN SHORTER.

I'VE BEEN MEANING TO ASK YOU.
WAS KOTOKO IWANAGA RIGHT ABOUT EVERY-THING?

YES.
KAORUKO-NÊSAN WANTED TO MARRY KÔYA-SAN...

...WITHOUT RUINING HIS BUSINESS, SO SHE SECRETLY DECIDED TO KILL MOM.

SHE DID THE LEG-BREAKING TRICK ALL ON HER OWN, TO CREATE AN ALIBI.
AND UNTIL RECENTLY, SHE'D KEPT IT FROM EVERYONE, INCLUDING KÔYA-SAN.

THEN DAD'S ASSIGN-MENT REVIVED THE PAST.
SHE ASKED KÔYA-SAN FOR HELP, AND HE OBLIGED...

WE SHOULD NEVER HAVE LET THAT HEIRESS GET IN-VOLVED.
WE KNOW FAR TOO LITTLE ABOUT HER.
SIGH...
I AGREE.
I NEVER WANT TO HAVE ANY-THING TO DO WITH HER AGAIN.

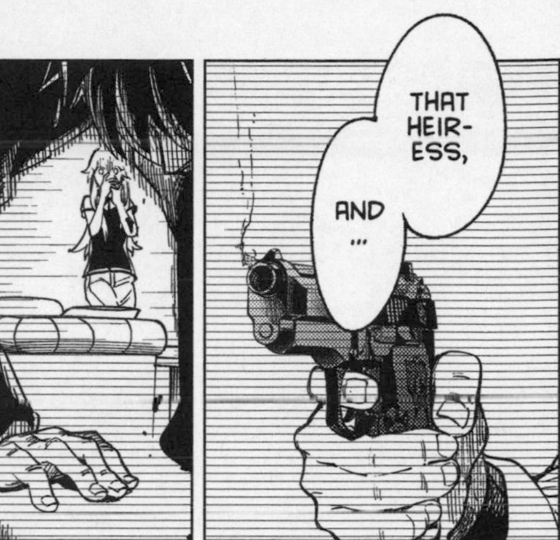
THAT HEIR-ESS,
AND ...

...THAT KURÔ SAKURA-GAWA PERSON.

I MEAN...

WERE THEY EVEN HUMAN?

NOW THAT THE SLEEPING MURDER HAS BEEN AWAKENED, THERE'S NO TELLING HOW LONG WE'LL BE DEALING WITH THE AFTERMATH.
THE SHADOWS HAVE ONLY GOTTEN DARKER AND THICKER.

I DIDN'T ASK YOU HERE TO RAIL AGAINST YOU.

I BROUGHT THESE RESULTS UPON MYSELF.
AND THEY WERE FULLY IN KEEPING WITH MY OWN CON-VICTIONS.
YOU MAY HAVE LACKED THE COMPASSION TO KEEP THE TRUTH LOCKED IN YOUR HEART,
BUT IT WOULD BE WRONG OF ME TO LAY THE BLAME ON YOU.

OH, I'LL LISTEN IF YOU DO WANT TO RAIL AGAINST ME.
I'M NOT THAT LACKING IN COMPASSION.
AND IT DOESN'T BOTHER ME.
I ASSUME YOU HAVE NO INTEREST IN WHAT HAPPENED AFTER YOU LEFT, AND I'M BREAKING OUR AGREEMENT BY ASKING YOU TO COME SEE ME.
BUT THERE IS ONE THING I JUST HAD TO KNOW.
KURÔ SAKURAGAWA-KUN, CORRECT?

I'VE HEARD THAT YOU ARE RIKKA SAKURA-GAWA'S COUSIN.
YOU KNOW RIKKA-SAN, SIR?
IT WAS SHE...
...WHOM I FIRST CONSULTED IN REGARD TO ATONING FOR MY CRIMES.
I HAD HEARD OF A CERTAIN HOSPITAL WHERE THEY WERE KEEPING AN IMMORTAL WOMAN WITH THE POWER TO DECIDE THE FUTURE.

I WAS TOLD THAT SHE DOESN'T USE HER ABILITIES TO GAIN POWER OR CONTROL PEOPLE,
BUT WHEN PEOPLE TALK TO HER, THINGS WOULD GENERALLY TURN OUT WELL FOR THEM.
THERE WERE RUMORS THAT THE HOSPITAL WAS HELPING HER RESEARCH A WAY TO BECOME A NORMAL HUMAN AGAIN.
AND THAT, IN EXCHANGE, SHE WAS USING HER POWERS FOR THEM.
I DON'T KNOW THE REAL REASON SHE WAS A LONG-TERM PATIENT OF THAT HOSPITAL.
BUT I HAD ONCE MADE A DEAL WITH A FOX SPIRIT.
SO HER STORY PIQUED MY INTEREST, REMINDING ME THAT EX-TRAORDINARY THINGS DO EXIST.
I ASKED HER ONCE TO MEET WITH ME.
AND SHE WAS THE REAL THING.

THOUGH SHE WAS BEAUTIFUL, IT WAS CLEAR TO ME THAT SHE WAS SOMETHING OTHER THAN HUMAN.
JUST TWO MONTHS AGO...
...I HAPPENED TO SPOT HER WALKING AROUND TOWN.
TAKE ME BACK TO THAT WOMAN.

I HAD BEEN TROUBLED ABOUT HOW TO DEAL WITH MY PAST CRIME, AND I SAW THIS ENCOUNTER AS DIVINE PROVIDENCE, SO I SPOKE TO HER.
I BELIEVED THAT IF MY PREDICAMENT WAS A RESULT OF INTERACTING WITH THE SUPERNATURAL, IT WOULD BE APPROPRIATE TO CONSULT A SUPERNATURAL BEING.
SHE DID HESI-TATE.
BUT SHE LISTENED TO ME.
HOWEVER, I DIDN'T TELL HER ABOUT THE MURDER.
I TOLD HER I HAD ONCE MADE A DEAL WITH A MONSTER, AND ASKED IF SHE KNEW A WAY I COULD ATONE FOR THE CRIME I HAD INSTIGATED.
OR IF PERHAPS SHE WOULD USE HER POWERS TO GET ME THE FUTURE I DE-SERVED.
THAT'S ALL I SAID TO HER.
AND SHE SAID...
FIND MY COUSIN— HE HAS THE SAME POWERS I DO. HE AND...

SHE TOLD ME THAT IF I WENT TO YOU, YOU COULD LIKELY GRANT MY REQUEST.
...

I HAD MY DOUBTS, BUT WHEN I DID SOME RESEARCH ON YOU, KOTOKO-SAN, I FOUND SEVERAL UNUSUAL ACCOUNTS.
THEN I MET YOU IN PERSON, AND I FELT AN UNUSUAL POWER.
BUT NEITHER OF YOU SEEMS VERY HUMAN TO ME.

IT MAY OFFEND YOU TO PUT IT THIS WAY,
CLENCH
THAT IS WHY I TRUSTED YOU WITH THIS MATTER.
BUT NOW THAT IT'S COME TO THIS, I CAN'T HELP BUT WONDER WHY I DID EXACTLY WHAT THIS RIKKA WOMAN TOLD ME, AND WHY I TRUSTED YOU.
HUFF
HUFF
SUD-DENLY I CAN'T BE SO SURE.

IS IT POS-SIBLE ...
...THAT RIKKA-SAN LED ME TO A FUTURE WHERE I FOLLOWED HER INSTRUCTIONS?
NEITHER SHE NOR KURÔ-SENPAI HAS THE ABILITY TO DREAM UP ANY FUTURE AND BRING IT TO THEM.
THEY CAN DO NO MORE THAN CHOOSE ONE FUTURE THAT ALREADY HAD A HIGH LIKELIHOOD OF OCCUR-RING.
WHEEZE
WHEEZE
YOUR PAST EXPERIENCE HAS MADE IT EASY FOR YOU, CHAIRMAN OTONASHI, TO TRUST SPECTRES.
AND YOU HAD A STRONG DESIRE TO SOLVE THIS MATTER, TOO, THROUGH THOSE SUPERNATURAL MEANS.
ALL RIKKA-SAN COULD HAVE DONE...
...WOULD BE TO ERASE ANY DOUBTS YOU HAD—THAT IS THE EXTENT OF HER ABILITY TO INTER-FERE.
SHE DOES NOT HAVE THE POWER TO MAKE YOU TO DO WHATEVER SHE WISHES.

I SEE.
YES.
I IMAGINE YOU'RE RIGHT.
DO YOU HAVE ANY IDEAS AS TO WHERE RIKKA-SAN IS NOW?
I HAVEN'T SEEN HER SINCE WE PARTED THAT DAY. WE DIDN'T EXCHANGE CONTACT INFORMA-TION, EITHER.
Heh...
I DOUBT SHE HAS ANY INTEREST IN THE OUTCOME OF THESE EVENTS.
BUT I WONDER IF SHE RECOMMENDED YOU TWO BECAUSE SHE FORESAW THIS CONCLUSION.
I DON'T KNOW.
ZSHHH
SHE IS A THORN IN MY SIDE, AS WELL.

I DON'T KNOW WHAT TO THINK ABOUT RIKKA-SAN PULLING THE STRINGS.

I *DID* FEEL THAT THE CHAIN OF EVENTS LEADING TO THE CHAIRMAN'S COMING TO ME WAS AWFULLY CONVENIENT.

BUT I HADN'T MANAGED TO GUESS THAT FAR.

ZSHHH

WHY DID SHE FORCE ME INTO THIS INCIDENT?

EVEN RIKKA-SAN COULDN'T HAVE PREDICTED THE TRUTH AND SEEN THE WHOLE EVENT FROM START TO FINISH BASED ON WHAT LITTLE INFORMATION HE GAVE HER.

DOZE

DOZE

MRK

MAYBE SHE'S ONLY TRYING TO TORMENT ME.

I CAN THINK OF TWO REASONS.

FIRST, MAYBE SHE WANTED TO KEEP YOU FOCUSED ON THIS CASE...
...SO YOU WOULDN'T NOTICE THAT SHE WAS GETTING READY FOR HER NEXT PLOT.
HMM.
THAT DOES SEEM MORE LIKELY THAN MERE HARASSMENT.

THE OTHER REASON ...
...IS TO SHOW ME HOW YOU SETTLE CASES THAT INVOLVE SPECTRES.

AFTER ALL OUR TIME TO-GETHER?
YOU'VE SEEN ME SETTLE THESE CASES HUNDREDS OF TIMES BY NOW.

THAT'S TRUE, BUT MAYBE BECAUSE THERE WERE HUMANS SO THOROUGH-LY TANGLED UP IN THIS CASE,
SHE THOUGHT THAT YOUR IDIOSYN-CRASIES WOULD BE MORE PRO-NOUNCED.

THIS TIME, YOU DIDN'T LET ANY EMOTION INTERFERE WITH RESTORING ORDER.
AND WE ALL COULD HAVE PREDICTED THE TRAGIC OUTCOME, BUT YOU EXPOSED THE TRUTH ANYWAY.

WHEN IT COMES TO PROTECT-ING ORDER, YOU SHOW NO MERCY.
MAYBE SHE FELT LIKE THIS WOULD MAKE THAT CLEAR TO ME.
H!!
ZSHHH
?
...
NO,
WAIT.
YOU MAKE ME SOUND LIKE A COLD, INHUMAN MACHINE.

IF ANYONE IS INHUMAN, IT'S CHAIRMAN OTONASHI.
HE NEEDED TO BE PUT IN HIS PLACE. EMOTIONS ARE IRREL-EVANT.
YEAH.
THAT'S HOW YOU SHOULD FEEL. YOU HAVE NOTHING TO WORRY ABOUT.
I'M NOT SURE YOUR BRAIN IS EVEN WIRED FOR WOR-RYING.
BOFF

WHEN YOU TALK LIKE THAT, *YOU'RE* THE ONE WITH NO EMOTION, KURÔ-SENPAI!
GRRRR

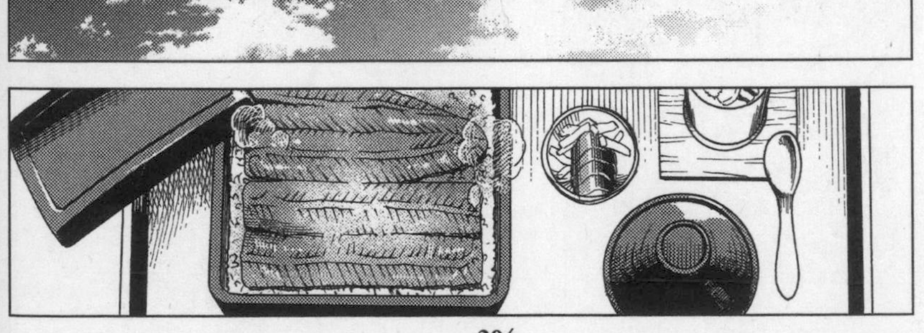

WALLA ガヤ
ぱん CLAP
WALLA ガヤ
WALLA ガヤ
ぱく CHOMP
OH, KURÔ.
HAVEN'T YOU FIGURED OUT YET JUST HOW AFRAID OF KOTOKO-SAN YOU SHOULD BE?

ZZZ
ZZZ
ZZZ
ZZZ
ZSHHH
TO BE CONTINUED IN VOLUME 12

IN/SPECTRE

A Very Respectable Afterword from the Author

I am the author, Kyo Shirodaira. And this is volume 11, with the conclusion of the "Sleeping Murder" case that started in the previous volume. It can be annoying to start the solution segment of a story and have it carry over into another volume, so I'm relieved that the conclusion made it into this one.

I'm sure many of you have realized, but the name of this arc comes from Agatha Christie's novel, *Sleeping Murder.* I think a direct translation into Japanese would be *Nemureru Satsujin.* It's a book about uncovering the truth behind an unsolved murder that had been dug up from the past and was sleeping in people's memories.

In Japan, such stories that deal with solving long unsolved cases, or cases that had been solved but new evidence casts doubt years later, are also called, "Murder in Memory" or "Murder in Retrospect," and you might say it's a standard premise for mysteries. Sometimes they're even called sleeping murder mysteries.

Because they happened so long ago, the only clues are the records kept and the memories of the people involved, and because the mystery went unsolved for so long, or is already presumed to be solved, it doesn't seem like the truth will be very easy to find. The records have already been pored over, leaving almost no room for any new interpretation, and people's memories have faded, while assumptions have grown stronger, and may have turned into a false understanding of the facts. And we can't count on new evidence or testimony. In light of all that, how will we reach the truth? Where is the key to solving the mystery? That's what makes this premise so interesting.

This time, I consciously tried to write a Christie-esque mystery, choosing the subgenre that the Queen of Mystery is said to excel at: the sleeping murder. It's a difficult premise to handle, because it tends to come across as dull and uninteresting, but on the other hand, because the case has already been examined so thoroughly, it's easy to present all the information needed to understand it in a compact format, and move the story forward quickly. In novels and manga, it's always best when you can get through those formalities without taking up too much time. Of course, for most of the cases in *In/Spectre*, the investigation is already almost over by the time Iwanaga gets involved, and one of the reasons for that is that I know it will speed things along.

But the mystery itself may have a lot of elements that are more reminiscent of Christie works other than *Sleeping Murder.* And there may be parts that remind you more of Chesterton or Crofts. And I think many of you have figured this out, too, but the name of the character Rion comes from a Shinichi Hoshi work. I've mixed all kinds of things in here.

A long case has ended in this volume, so expect the next volume to be a little more laid back. But we are steadily approaching the final showdown with Rikka-san.

I hope to see you again.

Kyo Shirodaira

Bonus Manga: DOPPELGANGER PARADISE

※NOTE: THIS MAY SPOIL THE MOOD OF THE LAST CASE, SO WE RECOMMEND THAT YOU TAKE TWO OR THREE DAYS AFTER THE MAIN STORY TO EITHER READ OR FORGET ABOUT THIS ONE.

HOW DO YOU DO, EVERYONE?
IN THIS INSTALLMENT OF END-OF-THE-VOLUME MANGA,
I WILL SNEAK UNDER SENPAI'S BED BEFORE HE GETS HOME FROM UNIVERSITY,
AND GIVE HIM A NIGHT-TIME CRAWLY SURPRISE!
KA-CHAK
NAN

CHANGE OF PLANS! TIME FOR A DAYTIME AVENTURA!
?!
WHAT ARE YOU DOING ?!
FWOO
YOU WILL TAKE THE AFTERNOON OFF TO DO THIS, THAT, AND THE OTHER THING WITH YOUR DARLING GIRLFRIEND!
NAA
OOOSH
~YÔKAI: CATCH-AND-DRAG-UNDER-THE-BED GIRL~
A YÔKAI THAT DRAGS HER INTENDED MALE UNDER THE BED. CAT-GIRL FOR SHORT.
FLAIL
THAT'S AN AWFULLY SHAMELESS ABBREVIATION!
COME!
COME!
FLAIL
LET GO OF ME!
THUD
UH.
TWO SENPAIS ?!

NOW LET ME CON-FIRM.
WHY DID EACH OF YOU COME HOME?
I WAS WORRIED THAT I'D FORGOT-TEN TO TURN OFF THE STOVE.
I WAS WORRIED ABOUT TURNING OFF THE STOVE, TOO.
YES, I SEE, I SEE.
NAN
NAN
WHEN A LIVING PERSON FEELS VERY STRONGLY ABOUT SOMETHING, PART OF THEIR SOUL WILL ESCAPE AS AN *IKIRYÔ*, OR LIVING GHOST, AND THEN POSSESS PEOPLE, APPEAR IN OTHER LOCATIONS, AND SO ON.
IN SOME CASES, THESE SPIRITS ARE IDENTIFIED AS THE SUPERNATURAL PHENOMENON KNOWN AS DOPPELGANGERS, IN WHICH SOMEONE SEES AN IDENTICAL COPY OF THEMSELF.
DURING CLASS, YOU WERE SO CONCERNED ABOUT THE STOVE,
Did I turn off the stove?
THAT YOU CREATED A LIVING GHOST.
THAT LIVING GHOST CAME HERE.
AND LATER, THE FLESH-AND-BONES SENPAI CAME HOME AS WELL.
It is bugging me. I'm going home.
YOU ARE BOTH MOST CERTAINLY KURÔ-SENPAI.
AND I CAN TOUCH SPIRITUAL ENTITIES, SO.
AHH, THIS IS HEAVEN.
NAN

YOU CREATED A LIVING GHOST OVER SOMETHING THAT POINT-LESS?
I'M ALREADY MIXED WITH YÔKAI.
MAYBE THE YÔKAI POWERS HAD SOME EFFECT ON MY BODY AND SPIRIT.

WELL.
THERE'S NO HARM IN IT.
IF YOU LIKE, I CAN PUT YOU BACK.
YEAH, PLEASE DO.

ALL RIGHT, GET A LITTLE CLOSER TOGETHER.
HERE GOES.
ONE, TWO...
ガッチャン
SMACK
THE PHYSICAL METHOD.

I'M BACK!
WELP.
GUESS I'LL MAKE LUNCH OR SOME-THING.
WAIT.
WHEW...
GOOD, GOOD.
DID I...
...JUST WASTE AN INCREDIBLE OPPORTU-NITY?
WAS THERE A REASON TO ERASE THE DOPPELGANGER RIGHT AWAY? COULD I NOT HAVE HAD A LITTLE MORE FUN WITH HIM FIRST?
YOU WANT SOME-THING TO EAT, IWA-NAGA?
WHAT? YOU'RE NOT HUNGRY?
RIGHT NOW...
...I AM THINKING VERY SERIOUSLY ABOUT HOW I COULD HAVE DONE THIS, THAT, AND THE OTHER THING AS A THREESOME!!
PLEASE REMAIN SILENT!
ギ GRG ギ GRG
ギ GRG ギ GRG ギ GRG
FIN

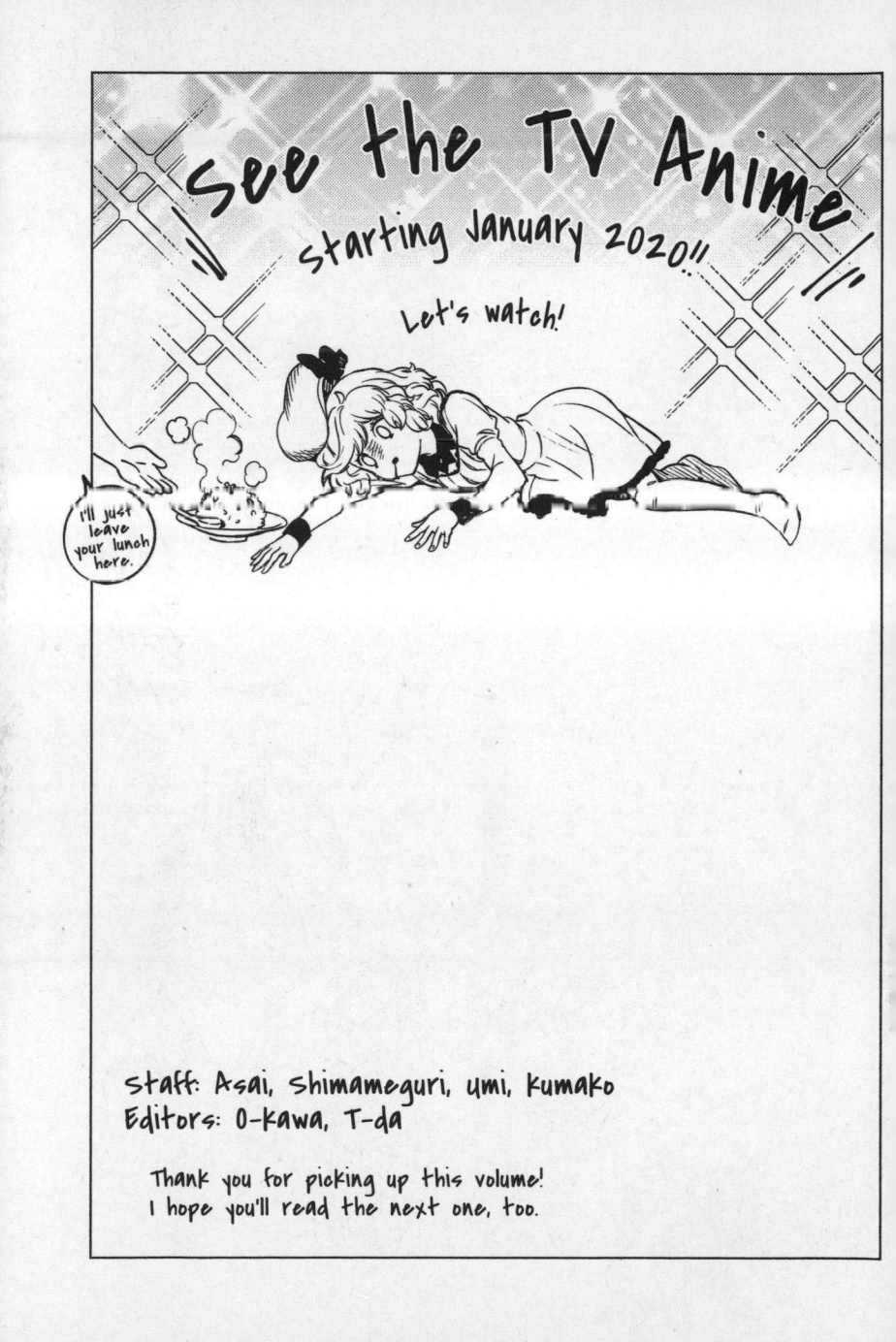

Staff: Asai, Shimameguri, umi, Kumako
Editors: O-kawa, T-da

Thank you for picking up this volume!
I hope you'll read the next one, too.

TRANSLATION NOTES

Tunnel wash, page 14

A more literal translation of the Japanese term Kotoko uses is "vase wash," where "vase (*tsubo*)" is a euphemism for a certain part of the female anatomy. A vase wash (or *tsubo-arai*) is a service provided at certain prostitution establishments where the woman has her customer hold up a finger and then proceeds to wash it inside her... vase.

Rion and lion, page 114

To be precise, Rion describes her name as a *romaji-yomi*, or Roman letter reading, of the English spelling of "lion." *Romaji* is the Japanese word for Roman alphabet—the letters we use in English—and is more specifically used in the context of writing Japanese words with Western characters. The name Rion is pronounced "ree-ohn" or "lee-ohn," as the sound often romanized as R is also the closest thing the Japanese language has to an L sound. As such, the name could also be spelled with an L, making the *romaji* for it "lion." The Japanese word for lion is *shishi*, but they usually use the English word, which is spelled in the Japanese writing system in characters that are romanized *raion*.

Murder being once done, page 121
The reader may be interested to know that this is the title of a murder mystery novel by Ruth Rendell.

Body sushi, page 130
As the name suggests, "body sushi" is sushi served on the body of a naked person. The Japanese term is *nyotai-mori*, which more literally means "served on the female body," but Kotoko is willing to reverse roles.

HAPPINESS

—ハピネス—

By Shuzo Oshimi

From the creator of *The Flowers of Evil*

Nothing interesting is happening in Makoto Ozaki's first year of high school. HIs life is a series of quiet humiliations: low-grade bullies, unreliable friends, and the constant frustration of his adolescent lust. But one night, a pale, thin girl knocks him to the ground in an alley and offers him a choice.

Now everything is different. Daylight is searingly bright. Food tastes awful. And worse than anything is the terrible, consuming thirst...

Praise for Shuzo Oshimi's *The Flowers of Evil*

A shockingly readable story that vividly—one might even say queasily—evokes the fear and confusion of discovering one's own sexuality. Recommended." —The Manga Critic

"A page-turning tale of sordid middle school blackmail." —Otaku USA Magazine

"A stunning new horror manga." —Third Eye Comics

A Kodansha Comics Trade Paperback Original

Published in the United States by Kodansha Comics, an imprint of Kodansha USA Publishing, LLC, New York.

Publication rights for this English edition arranged through Kodansha Ltd., Tokyo.

First published in Japan in 2019 by Kodansha Ltd., Tokyo as *Kyokou Suiri*, volume 11.

ISBN 978-1-63236-913-0

Original cover design by Takashi Shimoyama and Mami Fukunaga (RedRooster)

Printed in the United States of America.

www.kodanshacomics.com

9 8 7 6 5 4 3 2 1
Translation: Alethea Nibley & Athena Nibley
Lettering: Lys Blakeslee
Editing: Vanessa Tenazas
Kodansha Comics edition cover design by Phil Balsman

Publisher: Kiichiro Sugawara
Managing editor: Maya Rosewood
Vice president of marketing & publicity: Naho Yamada

Director of publishing services: Ben Applegate
Associate director of operations: Stephen Pakula
Publishing services managing editor: Noelle Webster
Assistant production manager: Emi Lotto, Angela Zurlo